BEFORE THE SUPREME COURT

The Story of Belva Ann Lockwood

Illustrated by
BEA HOLMES

by TERRY DUNNAHOO

BEFORE THE SUPREME COURT

The Story of Belva Ann Lockwood

1974
HOUGHTON
MIFFLIN
COMPANY
BOSTON

Library of Congress Cataloging in Publication Data

Dunnahoo, Terry.
    Before the Supreme Court.

    SUMMARY: A biography of Belva Ann Lockwood, fighter for women's rights, who
became the first woman to practice law before the Supreme Court and to plead the first
case for a Negro there.
    1. Lockwood, Belva Ann (Bennett), 1830–1917 — Juvenile literature. [1. Lockwood,
Belva Ann (Bennett), 1830–1917. 2. Lawyers] I. Holmes, Bea, illus. II. Title.
KF368.L58D8   340′.092′4 [B] [92]   73-22057
ISBN 0-395-18520-3

To my sister Jeanne
who knows of love and hope

Chapter One

"*Matthew, what is* the capital of France?" Belva Bennett asked one of her students.

The boy shuffled his bare feet and pulled at the hair that hung over his forehead. "It's . . . uh . . . it's . . ."

"It's not Royalton," a long, gangling youth said from the back of the room.

"I didn't ask you, Rufus. And stop whittling in class."

Rufus stilled his pocketknife. "Why do we have to know the capital of France? Albany will be the farthest any of us will get. You know that, Belva."

"While I'm teaching, you will call me Miss Bennett."

1

"Why, *Miss* Bennett? You're only fifteen like the rest of us."

"Students call teachers Miss or Mister. It's the rule," Belva said.

"How about Mrs.?" Rufus asked. He began to whittle again.

A girl said, "Rufus, you know married women aren't allowed to teach. Who would take care of their children?"

"I would, just so I wouldn't have to learn the capital of France."

The students laughed. It was summer and they were restless. But if they wanted to graduate, they had to spend the vacation months in class to make up work. The boys had left school to help with spring planting. The three girls had missed classes because of illness.

Belva called for attention. The students laughed louder. She clutched her book. Her voice rose. "Class, we are in the midst of a geography lesson." She walked toward Rufus. Several students stopped laughing. "It's a lesson I'm paid to teach, and it's a lesson I *will* teach." She took the knife from Rufus and slipped it into her dress pocket. She returned to her desk. "Now, Matthew, what is the capital of France?"

"I don't know, Miss Bennett."

One of the girls raised her hand. "It's Paris, ma'am."

"That's correct, Mary. Now who can tell me the

capital of Italy?" Rufus fingered the wood he had been whittling, but he didn't disturb the class again. When Belva dismissed the students, she gave Rufus his knife. "See you at the church picnic tomorrow, *Belva,*" he said.

On the way home, Belva clutched the drawstring purse that held her first week's salary. The money made Rufus's harassment tolerable. She didn't dislike Rufus. In fact, her friends suggested he was her beau. They thought it was romantic that both Belva and Rufus had been born on the same day — October 24, 1830. But Belva knew she could never marry Rufus. He had too little respect for school. The man she married would have to understand her need for learning.

Belva paused and looked up the road for Uriah McNall. Strange about Uriah. He had lived on the next farm all his life, but she had paid little attention to him until a barn raising last fall. She crossed the plank bridge that spanned the creek near her home. She didn't care if Rufus went to the picnic or not, but she hoped Uriah would be there.

Before Belva reached the house, her older sister Rachel ran out with the youngest child, Inverno, in her arms. "Let me see the money," Rachel said.

"It's in my handkerchief. I'll show you when we get inside."

The other two Bennett children played marbles on the floor, unimpressed by the fact that Belva was about to unwrap her first earned money. Her mother wiped her hands on her apron. "Did you get it? Did they pay you?"

"Of course they paid me," Belva said casually, but her excited fingers had trouble undoing the knot around the money. She pulled the cloth free. Rachel said, "Three silver dollars! Look, Mother, real silver dollars." She took one. Inverno reached for it. The coin fell from Rachel's hand and rolled across the room. A boot stopped it.

Belva looked from it to her father's sun-baked face. "The roof needs fixing," he said.

Hannah Bennett said, "Lewis, that money is for Belva's education at the academy in September. We agreed on it."

"You agreed on it, you and her. I only said I wouldn't stop her from teaching."

Belva loved her father. He was a good father, a good person, but to him education was for boys —sometimes. It was never for girls. "Father, I need that money for my tuition."

"What can they teach you at the academy? Algebra, philosophy, grammar? They'll do you no good when you're planting a crop or caring for a baby. You'll be married before you know it. What will your husband think of all this education?"

"I hope he'll think it will make me a better wife."

Lewis Bennett shifted his weight. The boot stayed on the coin. "That's crazy thinking. Look at your mother. The best wife a man ever had. Never went to school a day in her life."

Hannah Bennett said, "Lewis, the money is for Belva's education. I promised."

The boot moved a little. Belva went to her father. "Father, school is very important to me." He turned and walked out of the room. Belva picked up the coin.

"That was difficult for him, Belva," her mother said.

"Why is it so hard for a man to realize a girl should be educated?"

"It's always been that way," Mrs. Bennett said. Belva's mother had never mentioned her own lack of education. Belva wondered if she was sorry that she "never went to school a day in her life."

The roosters woke Belva the next morning. She looked through the uncurtained windows into the dawn. There wasn't a hint of sunshine. She got up and poured water from the pitcher into the washbasin. Rachel stirred behind her. "Is it your turn or mine to milk the cows?"

"It's mine." Belva wiped her face and hung the towel. Rachel turned on her stomach and pulled the

6

pillow over her head. Belva took it off. "You have to help in the kitchen. Mother said she would bake a pie for the picnic."

Rachel glanced at the window. "It looks like rain."

"It won't rain so get up and mix the dough." Belva put on a worn pinafore and buttoned it on her way through the kitchen.

"I suppose they'll have to call off the picnic," her mother said.

Belva opened the door and picked up the pails stacked outside. "The clouds will pass," she said.

The dew chilled Belva's bare feet. She ran to the barn. She opened the door and petted one of the cows. "I'm in a hurry this morning, Carrie," Belva said. She sat down and put a pail under the Guernsey.

Belva felt different about the picnic this year. She used to look forward to the races. She had won the girls' sack race the two previous years. Last year she had helped pull her side to victory in the tug-of-war game. But today she wouldn't enter the contests.

She remembered a couple of summers before when Rachel had stood aside and refused Belva's pleas to join her in the three-legged race. Belva couldn't understand then why her sister didn't want to take part in the games. Rachel had fingered her bonnet and smiled. Belva thought of Rufus and Uriah. She was glad she had a new bonnet.

When she finished the milking the sun was making a valiant attempt to take over the day. It was shining by the time the family finished breakfast. "I told you those clouds would go away," Belva said. She went to change her pinafore for the blue gingham dress she had made during the winter.

At the picnic grounds, the Bennetts stopped their wagon under an elm tree. Belva saw Rufus. He waved and aimed a slingshot at the bottle tied to a tree branch. He missed. Belva pretended not to notice. She helped the three smaller Bennett children from the wagon and looked for Uriah McNall.

Rufus came up beside her. "That's a pretty bonnet, Belva. You going to put it in the bonnet ring?"

Belva blushed. "I might," she said.

The minister called, "Time for the games, everybody." Rufus ran to him. Belva didn't move.

Her mother asked, "Aren't you going, Belva?"

"I don't think a schoolteacher should run a three-legged race," she said.

Her father asked, "All that education keep you from having fun?"

"Lewis, let's not have a fuss," Mrs. Bennett said. "I think our Belva is getting too old for such childish games."

"She thinks she's too smart for the likes of us, that's what it is."

8

Uriah's arrival at the picnic eased the sting of her father's words. Belva glanced toward Uriah several times, but he didn't look her way. She wondered if he knew she was there.

After the games, the minister said, "Now, young ladies, it's time for the bonnet ring." Rachel jumped to her feet. "Girls will put their bonnets in a ring for the young men to choose. Men, after you match the bonnet to the owner, you can share her lunch. You're in for a feast, lads. I've peeked and sniffed. There's some rare treats in those baskets. Come along girls."

Belva rose slowly. She took off her bonnet. She glanced at Uriah. He was talking to someone. Rufus watched her place her bonnet on the grass. She walked back to her family with Rachel. The minister said to the men, "When I drop my handkerchief, come choose a bonnet. But hurry, there are more of you than there are bonnets. I'm afraid some of you will go hungry unless you've prepared for such an emergency." The people laughed. Belva wished he would hurry.

The handkerchief dropped to the ground. Rufus ran for Belva's bonnet. A tall, slim man passed in front of him. He strolled toward Belva. "I believe this is yours, Miss Belva." Belva looked up into the smiling eyes of Uriah McNall.

Belva and Uriah were married three years later.

During that time she taught school in the summer and studied at the Royalton Academy during the winter. Uriah encouraged her. When people warned him about an educated wife, he said, "It makes her happy. A happy girl will make a good wife." After the wedding, people helped build a house for the newlyweds. Rufus came with his bride — one of the girls Belva had taught.

Uriah bought a sawmill, and Belva often measured lumber for customers while he ran the saw. Work filled her days. She milked the cows, fed the chickens, churned butter, planted crops. Occasionally, she wrote articles for the local newspaper and prepared papers for the literary gatherings in Royalton. Everyone said that Belva and Uriah made a good match.

Belva agreed. They were young and happy and healthy. But one morning Uriah woke with a cough he couldn't still. Belva said, "I'll ride out for the doctor."

"No, It'll stop. I'll be on my way to work in no time."

"You can't go like this, Uriah."

"I have to go. I have a big job at the sawmill." When the cough let up, Uriah ate and saddled his horse. He waved before he went around the bend in the road.

A short time later, Belva heard horses and a wagon. She ran outside. A man spurred his horse and stopped beside her. "It's Uriah, Belva. There's been an accident at the sawmill. We've sent for the doctor."

Belva ran to the wagon. Blood covered Uriah's head and face. She held his hand. It had the pallor of death. Someone said, "Here comes the doctor."

The man raced toward them. He jumped from his horse and examined Uriah. He turned to Belva. "It's no use, Mrs. McNall. His head is busted."

"Well, fix it then," Belva lifted her skirt and tore her petticoat. "Here, don't stand there. Bandage it up."

The doctor did as he was told. Then the men carried Uriah into the house and offered to do the chores. "There'll just be the milking tonight. If one of you will do that, I can stay with Uriah."

Neighbors came; her family came. For days Belva willed Uriah to live. He recovered slowly. One morning while the doctor examined him, Uriah had one of his coughing spells. The doctor put his ear to Uriah's chest. "How long has he coughed like this?" he asked Belva.

"For weeks, and it's getting worse."

The doctor waited until Uriah stopped coughing before he changed the bandage. He said nothing more about the cough.

Uriah gained strength. Some days he did a little work. Other days he was too sick to get out of bed. But slowly routine returned around the farm. A daughter, Lura, was born. She completed Belva's happiness.

Shortly after Lura's first birthday, Uriah began to have headaches. The coughing spells came more frequently. The doctor could do nothing. Five months later, on a cold, damp morning, Uriah died. At twenty-two Belva Ann McNall was a widow with an eighteen-month-old daughter to feed and clothe.

Mr. and Mrs. Bennett asked her to live with them. "No, I'll sell the farm and go back to teaching. I'll make do," she told him.

Soon after the funeral, dressed in widow's black, Belva went to the school trustees. One of the men paced in front of her. "Mrs. McNall, you realize it's highly unusual for a woman with a child to teach. Who will take care of your daughter while you're teaching other people's children?"

"My mother has offered to take care of Lura."

The man consulted with the others. He turned to her. "We're prepared to pay you three dollars a week."

Belva stiffened. "What do men teachers get?" she asked.

One of the trustees fingered his watch chain. "We're paying our men teachers eight dollars a week. But, of course, they have families to support."

Belva's blue eyes filled with anger. "Is my daughter

13

to go without needed clothes or food because I'm supporting her instead of her father?"

They moved uncomfortably. "That's our offer, Mrs. McNall. Will you take it?" the pacing man asked.

The man waited. "I'll have to think about it," Belva said.

She left the courthouse and walked past the blacksmith shop and the gristmill. She saw the minister's wife chopping wood. Belva told her what had happened. "It isn't fair," Belva said. "Why should men get more than twice as much money as women get for the same work?"

The woman leaned on her ax, "It's the way of the world, my dear."

"Then someone should change it."

"It can't be changed. It's always been like this."

Belva marveled at the woman's complete acceptance. "I'll change it," Belva said.

"You can't."

"I'll change it. At least I'll change it for me," Belva said. The minister's wife shook her head and went back to her woodpile.

Chapter Two

After she left the minister's wife, Belva went to the Bennett farmhouse. "I'm going back to school," she told her mother and Rachel.

Rachel asked, "Will you teach the next semester?"

"I'm not going to teach. I'm going to study."

Belva's mother stopped churning butter. "Belva, you're not serious."

"I am serious. I've decided women have to be better prepared for jobs in order to get them. I'm going back to the academy and eventually to college."

Her mother gasped. "Belva! Your father will never allow it."

"He has nothing to say about it. I'm old enough to make my own decisions."

Mrs. Bennett worked the churn again. Rachel said, "Women don't go to college."

"Then it's time they did," Belva said.

When Lewis Bennett heard about Belva's plans, he insisted she give them up. But Belva reminded her father he could no longer dictate to her.

"You'll disgrace the Bennett name," he told her.

"If my going to school disgraces a name, it will be the McNall name, not the Bennett name."

"You were born a Bennett."

"I'm sorry, Father, I won't change my mind," Belva told him.

Lewis Bennett's face tightened with anger. "Then you're a fool."

His words hurt, but they didn't alter Belva's plans. She entered the academy at the beginning of the term. When it finished, the village school needed a teacher for the winter semester. Belva asked for the job.

"Mrs. McNall, you know it's the policy of the school board to hire only men teachers for the winter session," one of the trustees told her.

"Do you have a male teacher?"

One trustee said, "We have several prospects."

Another said, "However, we'll need a teacher for the next summer session. Would you be interested in that?"

"At three dollars a week?" Belva asked.

"Of course," the man said.

Belva opened the door. "In that case, gentlemen, I'll return to school."

In December, a member of the school board came to the boarding house where Belva lived. "Mrs. McNall, may I speak to you a moment?" he asked.

"Of course," Belva said. She gave Lura a hug. "I'll read the book to you in a moment, dear. Here, sit beside me while I talk to the man."

They settled down on a worn love seat while the visitor sat on a wooden chair across from them. He cleared his throat. "Mrs. McNall, I've come to ask you to take over the winter session."

Belva felt a wave of triumph. "What happened to your male teacher?"

"Frankly, he didn't live up to our expectations. He couldn't discipline the class, and he had little knowledge of grammar. We had to let him go."

Belva leaned forward and faced the man directly. "If I accept, what will my salary be?"

The man perspired despite the coolness of the room. "Well . . . ahhh, well . . ." He rose from his chair. "We're prepared to give you eight dollars a week," he said.

Belva stood. "You may tell the school board I'm free to begin immediately." The man almost ran to the door.

Belva picked up Lura and danced with her around the room. "Your mother has won her first battle," she said. The little girl laughed. They whirled until they fell exhausted onto the love seat.

For a while Belva was happy with her teaching job. Her family was too. There was no more talk in the village about "that McNall woman." Everyone was pleased that at last she had found her sphere in life.

But as the weeks turned into months, Belva's obsession for more knowledge returned. One afternoon when she went for Lura, she found her mother alone. "Where's Lura?" Belva asked.

"She's playing on the old swing your father fixed for her."

Belva sat down across from her mother. "Mother, I want to go back to school."

Hannah Bennett stopped kneading the bread dough. "Why? Belva, what are you searching for?"

"I don't know, but I think the answer lies in advanced schooling. I'm going to enroll at Genesee Wesleyan Seminary. It's not college, but maybe it will satisfy my craving for learning."

"Genesee is sixty miles away. When would you see Lura?"

"On holidays and during vacations." Belva put her hand on her mother's arm. "Please, Mother, I must do this."

Her mother nodded. "Very well, I'll take care of Lura." Mrs. Bennett worked the bread dough again. She added, "And pray you won't ruin your life."

When Belva gave her resignation to the school board, the gossip about her started again. Her family tried to talk her out of going back to school. Rachel spoke to her in confidence. "How do you expect a respectable man to marry you if you continue to act this way?" she asked.

Belva laughed. "Rachel, I'm not being immoral. I'm merely going back to school."

No argument would change Belva's mind. And when Genesee Wesleyan Seminary in Lima, New York, opened its doors in September 1854, Belva sat in the front row of a political economy class ready to learn.

Belva missed her family, but she felt she had made the correct decision. In November she made another. She went to see President Cummings at Genesee College. "I want to transfer from the seminary to your school," she told him.

The man took the cigar from his mouth and flicked the ashes into the cuspidor. "I'm sorry, madam, we don't welcome females at our college."

"There have been women here in the past."

"Yes, and we've learned through those experiences that our studies are too difficult for most women."

"I'd like the opportunity to prove they're not too difficult for me," Belva said.

President Cummings puffed on his cigar. Belva moved to the edge of her chair. "I'll have to think about it," he said.

By the time Belva went home for Christmas vacation, he had grudgingly given her permission to enter the college at the end of the term. But she decided not to tell her family until the day she had to go back to Lima. The arguments and the constant reminder that the whole village was talking about her would have spoiled the holiday.

Before Belva packed, she examined her wardrobe. Her brown dress needed a new collar and the sole of her right shoe was thin. Her cape was threadbare. But she couldn't afford new clothes.

Tuition at the college was eight dollars and fifty cents a term — a bit more expensive than the seminary. And there was an added charge of a dollar twenty-five cents for cutting and carrying wood to her room. And there had to be money to pay her mother.

Belva made a budget. If she wanted to graduate, she would have to get through college in three years instead of four.

With this in mind, Belva let little distract her. She took more than the required courses and studied until "lights out." She didn't let up until the day she heard several men students talk about Susan B. Anthony. "That bloomer girl is making a speech at the inn this evening," one of the students said to the man beside him.

"She should be locked up for the things she's trying to get women to do. Her and that Elizabeth Stanton. And there's another one — Lucy Stone, I think her name is," one of the men said.

"Yes, that's it. They're trying to get the vote for women. What do women know about politics?"

Belva bit her lip. She wanted to tell them that women knew a lot about politics, but she held her temper. Students weren't allowed off campus at night, and she didn't want to arouse the men's suspicions. But she had to hear Susan B. Anthony. Belva had read about the equal rights movement since its first meeting in Seneca Falls, New York, in 1848 — the year she had married Uriah.

Belva went to her room and tried to think of a way out of the building. If she left from the front door, one of the men would see her. If she used the back door, the servants would ask her where she was going. She looked out the window. There was a tree. Belva judged the distance between it and the building. It was too far.

She walked through the halls. On the main floor, she found a door she hadn't noticed before. She opened it and went down the stairs into the cellar. A window unlatched at her touch. She wondered if she could find her way to it in the dark. She had to. She returned to her room until time to go out.

When she went back to the cellar, darkness engulfed her. She almost changed her mind about going to the inn. But curiosity urged her on. She felt her way along the wall to the window. She climbed out and ran down the dirt road. She waited in the shadows of the inn. When she saw no one she recognized, she entered the dining room.

Chairs had been arranged in rows. At a table in the front of the room stood a tall, slim woman dressed in gray. Her hair was parted in the middle and smoothed over her ears. She was a portrait of flawless grooming. Miss Anthony's appearance surprised Belva. From the descriptions in the papers of women in the equal rights movement, she had expected an ill-kempt woman dressed in bloomers. There had been so much written about the long, full trousers under the short flared skirt and the women who wore them that Belva hadn't thought of Susan B. Anthony as a woman much like herself.

The speaker began. Her voice was soft and un-trained. She was obviously nervous. But as she warmed to her subject, her eyes sparkled. Her voice grew stronger. "Wives must become equal partners with their husbands," she told her audience. "Women must demand change so one day they can work in shoe shops, dry goods stores, law offices, any place where men are now kings." She talked for more than an hour. When she finished, there were boos and catcalls, but there was applause too. Belva was surprised and pleased that much of the applause came from men.

Back in her room, she lay in the darkness unable to sleep. Could women get jobs in shops and offices? If they could, maybe they could get jobs in the pro-fessions. Women doctors, women architects, or women lawyers sounded impossible. Yet, if women wanted it badly enough it could be.

Belva remembered her mother's question, "Belva, what are you searching for?" She turned over in bed. She didn't know. She had started a scientific course, because it was something she wanted to take. Now she asked herself why. She didn't feel capable of being a doctor. But she did like law. And teaching had its advantages. She could reach young minds. She could help young ladies to think for themselves, to assert their independence. Belva slipped into an uneasy sleep before she decided what she would do.

By June she still hadn't reached a decision, but she was more determined than ever to get a degree from Genesee. Before she left for Royalton to spend her vacation with her family and Lura, she learned this might be possible. Her work had been so satisfactory, she would pass into the junior class in September instead of the sophomore class. If she continued to watch her pennies, she would have enough money to graduate. She went home to tell her family the news. But the Bennetts had news of their own. They were moving west.

Her father told her. "I hear there's a lot of new things opening up out there. I want to get in on some of them."

"What about the farm?"

"I have a buyer."

"You'll be so far away." Panic gripped Belva. "I'll never see you."

"You can give up your crazy ideas and come with us."

"I can't stop now."

Her mother asked, "How can you continue with no one to take care of Lura?"

Belva searched her mind for an answer. There was none. "When are you going?" she asked.

"In the fall, after the crops are in," her father said.

Belva was relieved. There was time for them to change their minds.

The Bennett children and Lura were caught up in the excitement of traveling on a train. They talked of little else. Several times Belva tried to tell Lura she wasn't going with the Bennetts, but the child was too excited to listen.

One night after the others were asleep, Hannah Bennett asked Belva, "Have you decided what you'll do with Lura?"

Belva shook her head. "Nothing is acceptable. I can give up my studies. I can stay in college and let strangers care for her. Or . . ." the words stuck in her throat. "Or I can let her go with you and not see her for two years."

"She'll be welcomed with us, but think about it hard, Belva. Would a piece of paper from a college be worth the loneliness?"

Belva clenched and unclenched her hands. "I've thought of little else all summer. And every time I'm ready to give up and go with you, I think of what Susan B. Anthony said about women changing things. Mother, there's a world full of things women can have, if they want them badly enough."

Hannah Bennett went to Belva and hugged her. "I'll leave you to think. You have to make this decision alone."

Belva turned down the lamp and sat in the dark. The church bell in the village tolled ten o'clock. It was dawn before she decided she would stay in college and let Lura go west.

In August, surrounded by her family, Belva found that decision acceptable. But when the day came for her to return to college, she had to talk to herself, argue with herself, force herself to go. She hugged her mother and held Lura until the carriage driver called impatiently. Belva climbed in. The carriage lurched forward. She waved until it turned the bend in the road. Then she let the tears come.

Chapter Three

*B*elva *had to take* the classes she had missed by skipping her sophomore year. These, added to the regular junior-year studies, kept her so busy she had little time to think about her family. But holidays, with no regularly scheduled classes, were wretched. Christmas was unbearable, the summer vacation endless. She thought often of giving up and taking a train west.

But when she returned for her senior year, it was with fresh determination to graduate and an unexpected opportunity to study law in the village. Unfortunately, since the class wasn't connected with Genesee College, she would have to use part of her reserve funds to pay the entrance fee. She counted her money. She made another budget. If she allowed herself nothing but the simplest necessities, she could manage. She enrolled with several men students from Genesee.

The class both fascinated and angered her. She liked to prepare practice cases. She liked to plead her "case" before a make-believe jury. But sometimes the professor's lectures moved her to speak out against the inequality of the law.

"It's a man's law, made by men, enforced by men and decided by men," she told him one morning.

"But the law protects women as well as men," the professor said.

Belva couldn't accept that. "Professor, after marriage, what happens to property a woman owned before the ceremony?"

"It becomes her husband's property," the professor said.

"Exactly. And when the husband dies, he is allowed to will it to his eldest son. The wife is left without property. Often she's at the mercy of a selfish son and daughter-in-law."

"That would be an unusual case," the professor said.

"Perhaps. But you can't deny the law is unfair to women." The teacher started to say something. Belva interrupted. "And another thing, a woman can work from dawn until dark while her husband stays home in a drunken stupor. Yet, the law allows the man to take her salary and spend it on more liquor while his wife and children go hungry."

One of the students asked, "Is that true, Professor?"

Belva answered for the teacher. "I know it's true. I've seen it happen. And can you believe the children don't even belong to the wife? A husband can throw his wife out of the house and keep their children, and she has no legal recourse." Belva asked her teacher, "Do you still say the law is equal for men and for women?"

"But these are unusual cases, Mrs. McNall," the professor repeated. His hands gestured his uneasiness. "And a woman can get help if she seeks it."

"Sometimes she can. But when it comes to the final decision, these are the laws, and men enforce the laws."

The dismissal bell rang. The students didn't leave. Finally, the professor said, "You have a point, Mrs. McNall. Perhaps we can discuss it at the next session." Belva walked from the room, straight and tall. She had made a point, and the men had listened. She liked the feeling.

Belva's busy class schedule helped her senior year pass quickly, but it didn't ease her loneliness. As June 1857 approached, and with it graduation, she made no plans except plans to go to her family after classes ended.

One evening Belva was studying for final exams when she heard footsteps. There was a knock. "Yes?" Belva said.

The matron opened the door. "President Cummings wishes to see you in his office," she said.

Belva tensed. President Cummings never sent for anyone unless there was trouble. She dashed past the matron. When Belva reached the office, her hand hesitated on the doorknob. She turned it and entered. President Cummings rose. He was smiling.

"Ah, Mrs. McNall, come in, please." He gestured toward the chair beside his desk. Belva sat down. President Cummings eased his ample body into his chair. "Mrs. McNall, you're the new preceptress of the Lockport Union School District. I recommended you. You'll start right after graduation," he said. Belva stared at him, stunned. "What's the matter, Mrs. McNall? Don't you want the position? Why anyone would want it."

Belva spoke slowly. "I can't accept it. That's why I didn't apply. I'm going west the day I graduate."

"Good heavens, what's in that savage country that would permit you to even think of turning down this opportunity?"

"My daughter, Lura," Belva said simply.

President Cummings' face softened. "Oh, yes, of course, I forgot. But can't you bring her here?"

"Transportation being what it is, it would take weeks. And . . ." Belva hesitated. "Frankly, sir, I don't have the money for the return trip."

"You're not going to stay there? What would you do?"

"I'll take a job while I look for something I like. If I don't find anything, I'll stay until I can save enough money to come back east."

"Mrs. McNall, surely you can't turn down this Lockport offer. Within months you could earn enough to go for your daughter and bring her back. She would have the benefit of one of the finest schools in New York."

Belva said, "I don't understand, President Cummings. Why did you recommend me? When I came to you, you were certain I couldn't complete your college courses."

President Cummings moved uncomfortably. "You've proven me wrong. You've made the most of every opportunity. Lockport would be fortunate to have you." He leaned toward her. "Please reconsider. You would be turning down a position with prestige and an excellent salary."

"I've been away from my little girl so much, President Cummings."

He stood. "I won't say anything to the school officials in Lockport. You think about it a few days.

Think of the benefits to your daughter's education and to your future together. This position represents everything you've worked for."

Alone in her room, Belva didn't know if the job was everything she had worked for, but President Cummings was right about Lura. Lockport would allow her to receive the kind of education Belva had wanted for herself. Belva paced the worn flowered rug in her room. "A few months. A few more months," she thought. Darkness came. She didn't go down to dinner. She prepared for bed, but she couldn't sleep. She got up and put on her wrapper. She turned up the gas lamp and found her pen. She hoped Lura would understand.

Mail delivery from the West was slow. It was weeks before Belva got a letter from her mother that said Lura was disappointed at not seeing Belva, but she was excited about the idea of living in the East. The letter completed Belva's growing confidence that she had made the correct choice.

Belva lived frugally. She saved almost every penny of her salary. Just before Christmas she went for Lura and brought her back to Lockport. It was Belva's happiest Christmas in years.

The Lockport School was known throughout the Northeast for its high standards. Lura, now six years old, joined the seven hundred students in a progressive program Belva labored tirelessly to improve. She met with parents to urge change in the curriculum. She listened to students' problems. She became active in local and state school associations. At one of the meetings she met the woman she had sneaked out of Genesee College to hear. She walked to the stage where Susan B. Anthony waited to begin her talk and introduced herself. "Miss Anthony, I'm Belva McNall," she said. "And I want to help."

After that encounter, the two women saw each other often at one meeting or another. One evening, after a difficult session of speeches and debates, Belva stayed to help Susan tidy the hall. "You made a good speech this evening, Susan," she said.

"I should have been more forceful," Susan said. "I wish I had learned to speak before an audience when I was younger. I would be more effective now." She stopped sweeping. "Public speaking should be added to girls' school programs. They would gain confidence and poise from it."

Belva said, "I could do it at Lockport."

"You'll run into opposition. There aren't many parents who will allow their daughters to speak in public. Remember it's 'shameful, demeaning and, above all, unladylike.' "

Belva said, "I think it's worth a try. Let's bring it up at the next meeting." Susan nodded and began to sweep again. Belva stacked chairs. She wished they had money to hire someone to clean up after meetings.

When Belva and Susan introduced the public-speaking issue at the next meeting, opposition came from almost everyone. But Belva and Susan had prepared themselves well. They won most of the arguments. Before the evening ended, they received permission to establish a temporary public-speaking program and report on it at the end of the first school quarter.

Belva introduced the program in her school the next day. Before evening, the father of one of her students threatened to go to the school board and demand her resignation.

"I have permission to teach public speaking," Belva told him.

The man's voice rose, "I'll remove my daughter from your school rather than expose her to jeers and ridicule."

Belva tried to reason with him, but he wouldn't listen. He said, "My daughter will leave and so will all the others. I'll see to that." He stomped to the door. "Girls should be home mending and cleaning, not making spectacles of themselves." The man pulled open the door and slammed it shut behind him. Belva stared at it. She knew this was the first of many visits.

Despite the objections, Belva continued the program. She taught speech writing, voice training and the importance of delivery. The students were enthusiastic. They could hardly wait to appear before an audience. But when the time came, they fidgeted, they stammered, one of them threw up. When the ordeal finished, the girls said they couldn't do it again. Belva insisted they could.

The girl who had been sick started to cry. "I was so afraid," she said. She was pale from her ordeal.

Belva put her arm around the girl's shoulder. "Everybody is afraid sometimes. But if you keep doing things, if you keep trying, it becomes easier."

The girl wiped her eyes. "You mean I won't be afraid anymore?"

Belva looked at her and at the other girls who waited for her to give them a magic formula. She wished she had one. "I didn't say that. I said it would become easier. Will you try?" One by one the girls said they would. "Thank you," Belva said.

Every Saturday afternoon, each girl gave a short speech to an audience. They still fidgeted and stammered, but as the weeks passed their poise and confidence improved. Most parents were pleased. When Belva and Susan gave their report at the end of the school quarter, the program won approval.

The talk at these school meetings was naturally about education. And the discussions at the women's suffrage meetings Belva attended with Susan were usually about the rights of women. But slowly, without anyone being aware of it, much of the talk turned to war — a civil war, a war between the states.

When the war came, Belva organized the girls of the Lockport School District into classes to make clothes, bandages and lint for the soldiers. She packed these with presents that members of the Women's Aid Society prepared and sent them to distribution centers. As preceptress of the Lockport School and president of the society, it was her duty to help the men of Lockport who marched to battle. But as a citizen of a country she loved, she protested the war. She believed that war was wrong, always wrong. And she didn't hesitate to say it at every opportunity. Unfortunately, not everyone shared her views.

One day the president of the school board sent for her. "Mrs. McNall, I must ask you to stop your talk against the war," he said.

"I can't," Belva told him.

Shocked, the man asked, "You can't believe slavery is acceptable?"

"The black man must be free," she said. "I don't object to that. What I object to is the method of freeing him."

"President Lincoln needs our help. Our men need our help."

"And I will help them in every way I can. But that

doesn't change my opinion about the war."

The man sighed with resignation. "Very well. You're entitled to your opinion. But as one of our teachers, you'll have to promise not to express it openly."

"I can't promise that."

The man stood up. He towered over her. "You must, or I'll have to ask for your resignation."

"You'll have it in the morning," Belva said. She went out and slammed the door shut behind her. Anger filled her thoughts. But before she reached home, worry replaced that anger. How would she and Lura manage? But Belva wouldn't reconsider. She had to speak out for what she felt was right. She would tender her resignation in the morning.

Through the summer of 1861, Belva read about the war. There were skirmishes along the coast. In July there was a battle at Bull Run in Virginia. Belva shuddered at the list of casualties. She questioned the appointment of General George B. McClellan as commander of the Union army. She felt helpless.

In September she took charge of the Female Seminary in Ganesville, New York. Lura, now eleven, adjusted quickly to the new school. One evening Belva asked her, "What do you think I should add to the program first, higher mathematics, public speaking or calisthenics?"

"Why don't you introduce them all at once?" Lura asked.

"Parents. I have to get them to accept one thing at a time."

"Then do the calisthenics first. The girls really liked that at Lockport."

Belva chuckled. She remembered the way the students had refused to do even a knee bend, and how they balked at lying on the floor to firm the stomach muscles. Finally Belva did the exercises. The students giggled, but they joined her on the floor. Eventually calisthenics became their favorite class. Belva looked at Lura. Her body was slim and strong. Belva said, "We'll do the calisthenics. A healthy mind needs a healthy body."

Unfortunately the owner of the seminary didn't agree with her. When Belva presented the idea to her the next morning, she was shocked. "Calisthenics make people perspire, Mrs. McNall. Proper young ladies do not perspire."

And so, Belva had to be satisfied with higher mathematics, at least for the time being. She hoped to work public speaking and calisthenics in later, but she didn't get a chance. The main building of the seminary burned to the ground after she'd been there a year, and she found herself unemployed once more.

She took a job teaching at Hornellsville, but her

views about the war and her belief that girls should get as thorough an education as boys didn't harmonize with the views of those in charge there. She gave her resignation and with money she had saved from her salary, opened her own seminary in Oswego, New York, where she could prepare young ladies for the future.

The war continued. There had been another battle at Bull Run, and one at Fredericksburg. Then there was Gettysburg. Belva wondered if the fighting would ever end. She read about the destruction left by Sherman's march through Georgia. Surely, there would be a truce now. But the battles continued. Finally, General Robert E. Lee surrendered to General Ulysses S. Grant on April 9, 1865. The war was finished. Belva told her students there would never be another war. The country would begin to grow again. It would prosper. It would be a sane place to live. Five days later, she read the headlines: LINCOLN SHOT.

Distressed by the news, she wondered how she could help. She thought about it for weeks and finally decided that she could do little in Oswego. She asked Lura, "How would you like to live in Washington?"

"What is there for us in Washington?"

Belva looked at her daughter. Her brown hair hung past her shoulders. Her blue eyes sparkled like her father's. Her skin was flawless. At sixteen she was a beauty. "I don't know. But we'll never find out unless we go see. What do you think?"

"I think it's a marvelous idea," Lura said.

Belva took her pen and wrote a "for sale" notice for the McNall Seminary of Oswego, New York.

Chapter Four

During the trip from Oswego to Washington, Belva thought of her new life with Lura. The sale of the seminary had brought little money, but she didn't regret her decision. Now she could give up teaching. Surely a city that housed Congress, the Supreme Court and the President of the United States had exciting jobs for women. But when she reached Washington and searched the papers for "situations available," she found she could be a maid, a companion to an elderly lady, or a teacher.

When she expressed her disappointment to Lura, Lura said, "You don't have to begin work right away, Mother. We have the money from the seminary to keep us going until you find something you want to do."

"We have to save that in case one of us gets sick."

Lura said, "Perhaps I can get a job."

"You can go back to school. There will be no maids or companions to elderly ladies in this family as long as I can teach," Belva said. She picked up the Washington *Star* and read one of the ads: "Wanted — Assistant — Miss M. J. Harrover's Young Ladies Seminary, 13th St. West between G and H." Belva reached for her muff. "You unpack. I'll go see Miss Harrover. When I get back, we'll look over our new city."

Miss Harrover was a short, plump woman who wore an out-of-date hoop skirt that made the bottom part of her body look like an inflated ball. She smiled when Belva entered. Her pleasure turned to delight when Belva told her about her previous work. "That's excellent, Mrs. McNall. My young ladies will be fortunate to have you."

"May I ask the salary?" Belva said.

Miss Harrover played with the brooch at her neck. "Of course, you will teach only until one o'clock. The rest of the day will be yours to do as you please."

Belva knew immediately the salary wouldn't be in line with her experience. "I'm supporting myself and my daughter. I have to have enough to live on," she said.

"The salary is fifteen dollars a week," the woman said. Belva rose to leave. Living was expensive in

Washington. Fifteen dollars a week would hardly pay the rent and buy necessities. Miss Harrover said, "Naturally, your daughter may attend the school free of charge."

Belva sat down again. "May I see the curriculum?" she asked.

Miss Harrover took a folder from her desk. Belva studied the papers. The courses proved satisfactory for the moment. "I can begin tomorrow," she said.

Miss Harrover smiled. "You have made a wise decision, Mrs. McNall."

Belva didn't agree, but she felt it was the only reasonable decision she could make.

At the boarding house, Belva told Lura the job was a temporary thing. "But Washington isn't. Let's go see it," she said.

Lura put on her coat and bonnet. She pushed a wisp of hair into place and tied the ribbons under her chin. She picked up her gloves. "I'm ready," she said.

A mild breeze ruffled their skirts. The sun warmed their faces. "I wonder if this is normal February weather in Washington," Belva said. A moment later a coal delivery wagon passed them. She decided that the day wasn't typical.

Lura said, "This street looks as though a giant had mixed big houses with little ones, then threw them out to see how they would land. Look at the small house next to that mansion And look over there. Certainly no one would build a city this way on purpose."

Belva said, "Except for the part Major L'Enfant planned in 1791, I'm afraid Washington was built willy-nilly."

They walked up Pennsylvania Avenue toward the Capitol that dominated the hill. Belva grew more determined that her teaching would be temporary. Washington was the political center of the country. There had to be something besides teaching for her here.

From the Capitol they went to the White House. A carriage came down the drive and turned onto the avenue. Lura said, "I couldn't see who was inside. Do you think it was President Andrew Johnson?"

Belva laughed. "I don't know, but if we're going to live in Washington, I suppose we'll learn not to stare into carriages."

She turned toward the Washington Monument. "Let's go see it. I read work on it might begin again now that the war is over."

Lura said, "I hope they do something. These sheds are horrible. What do you suppose is in them?"

Belva looked at the white obelisk, then at the weather-beaten sheds. "I don't know," she said.

A sweeper leaned on his broom. "Those sheds hold the rest of the blocks for the monument," he said.

Belva gasped. "But those were gifts from royalty all over the world! They were given to the people of America for a monument, not to be kept in dirty, old buildings."

"There's talk about finishing the monument," the man said.

"I know and I think I'll find out when," Belva said.

The man tipped his hat and began to sweep again, "Yes, ma'am," he said.

Belva and Lura went from the Washington Monument to the House of Representatives Office Building, to the Library of Congress and to the Supreme Court. Before they started back to the boarding house, Belva resolved to spend much of her time in these buildings.

At one o'clock the following day, while Lura struggled with geometry, Belva rode in a horse-drawn cart to the Supreme Court Building where the guard told her Court was not in session. Disappointed, she hurried up the hill to the Capitol. She climbed the stairs to the visitor's gallery. Senators — tall, short, whiskered, stooped, old and young — sat below her.

Many of them read newspapers. One took a snuff box from his pocket. Another glanced at the galleries and waved to someone in the crowd. Others gave their attention to the man delivering a speech. When he finished, several senators jumped to their feet.

A gavel pounded. Someone said, "The chair recognizes Senator Trumbull from Illinois."

The others sat down. A tall, gray-haired man stood alone. A few senators put down their papers. Others sat up in their chairs. Senator Trumbull cleared his throat. His words reached the gallery easily. Still, Belva leaned forward. He talked about freedom, about the right of citizenship, about the right to vote. He spoke a long time. Senators moved impatiently. Some began to read again. Senator Trumbull's words continued. He paced as he spoke. Finally, he stopped moving. He looked around at his fellow senators. "Gentlemen, I say that all persons born in the United States must be declared citizens, and all citizens of every race and color must enjoy equal rights in every state and in every territory of the United States."

Applause and hisses exploded in the gallery. Belva joined the applause. The gavel pounded. "Clear the galleries. Clear the galleries," the chairman said. Suddenly Belva was quickly and unceremoniously ushered out the door.

This was her first experience with the workings of the government. After that, almost every afternoon, Belva listened to debates in Congress and arguments in the Supreme Court. She studied the art, the geology and the geography of the surrounding country. She spent hours in the Library of Congress reading congressional records. And she joined a group of women fighting for equal rights.

The women were in the midst of a major battle. Congress had drafted a fourteenth amendment. It read in part: ". . . when the right to vote at any election for the choice of electors for President and Vice-President of the United States, representatives in Congress, the executive and judicial officers of a State, or the members of the legislature thereof, is denied to any of the male inhabitants of such state . . ."

Belva and her group wanted one word struck from the amendment. The word "male." They wrote letters; they held meetings; they protested. But they lost. In June 1866, Congress passed the Fourteenth Amendment over President Andrew Johnson's veto and sent it to the states for ratification. If the amendment became law with the word male in it, women would have more trouble getting the right to vote. While Susan B. Anthony and Elizabeth Stanton made speeches in the North against the amendment, Belva and other women in the District of Columbia worked to get the offensive word deleted.

Despite her grueling schedule, Belva searched the "situations wanted" section of the Washington *Star* every day for another position. She answered every offer that looked promising. But after five months, she was still at Miss Harrover's.

She was discouraged and angry. One evening during dinner she told Lura, "I can't wait for a suitable job any longer. I'm going to create one."

Lura put down her fork. "How does a person create a job?"

"By going into business. I looked at the Union League Hall on Ninth Street today. I'm going to buy it."

"Why?" Lura asked.

Belva buttered her bread. "Because it's a good investment. There's several halls I can rent for meetings. There's room for a small school. There's even an apartment on the third floor we can live in." Belva took a bite of her bread.

Lura said, "Women rent rooms in their homes to make money, but isn't renting halls a strange business for a woman?"

"It's strange only because women don't do it. But if men won't give me suitable opportunities to support myself, I'll make them. I'll give my notice to Miss Harrover tomorrow."

Within a short time Belva and Lura had moved into the apartment on Ninth Street, and Belva started a school that offered girls the same curriculum presented in the best boys' schools. Belva reasoned that if she *had* to teach, she would teach a progressive program.

One day, early in 1867, she had to interrupt her class to show the halls and discuss rates with women from the Temperance Society. When Belva returned to her students, Lura had taken over. Belva listened. She was amazed at her daughter's ability to handle a class. After that, Lura taught more and more often while Belva attended to her rental business.

Neighbors snubbed her. Belva's work wasn't proper women's work, and they let her know it. She was upset by the treatment, but she hoped to change their minds by eventually convincing them that a woman could do a man's job.

Although her neighbors' abuse hurt her, it didn't compare to the abuse she experienced from hecklers at the women's equal rights meetings. The verbal attacks were often so vicious, she had to fight the urge to run off the stage. One evening she ended a meeting when she was struck by a cabbage thrown from the audience. After the hall was cleared, Belva asked the speakers, James and Julia Holmes, to stay. The Holmes's had vacationed in Colorado not long before, and Julia had climbed Pike's Peak — the first white woman to reach the top.

The three of them sat around the kitchen table with hot chocolate. Belva said, "If I weren't so convinced that women must take their place in society, I would never attend another meeting."

James Holmes took a sip of his hot chocolate. "What can we do?" he asked. "We can't keep out hecklers. We're not certain who is for our cause and who is against it until they're inside. Then it's too late."

Belva said, "We need to organize so we'll know who we can count on. But we can't get anything done at the hall."

Julia asked, "Why don't we invite people we trust to come to our house? We can ask for suggestions and decide what to do."

"That's a good idea," Belva said. "I'll send letters in the morning. Let's hope tonight hasn't discouraged anyone."

A small group gathered at the Holmes's residence the following week to talk about forming an equal rights association. Before the meeting ended they agreed the idea needed more discussion. But they made definite plans about future gatherings. Although many of the meetings were degrading, they would be kept open to the public. The police would be sent for if the crowd became too rowdy. And the group for women's equal rights would welcome press coverage. As Senator Samuel C. Pomeroy said, "Any publicity is good publicity when you're trying to get your ideas to the public."

The group met again the evening of July 5, 1867, in the Washington Building at the intersection of Pennsylvania Avenue and C Street. Belva didn't feel like going. It was hot and humid. Her clothes clung to her as soon as she put them on. But there would be more talk about organizing, and she had promised to be there.

When she entered the Washington Building, a tall, thin man welcomed her. "I'm Ezekiel Lockwood, and you are Belva McNall," he said.

Belva was flattered he knew who she was. "It's kind of you to let us hold our meeting in your dental office," she said.

"The group is welcome anytime," Dr. Lockwood said.

The meeting had few interruptions, and there was progress in the plan for an association that would hold them together. Belva was glad she had come. When the meeting adjourned, James and Julia Holmes offered to escort her home.

Dr. Lockwood said, "Nonsense, you two go along. I'll see that Mrs. McNall gets home safely." He turned to Belva. "That is if you don't mind, madam."

Belva smiled, "I hate to put you through any trouble."

Dr. Lockwood took his hat from the hall tree. "No trouble at all, Mrs. McNall. It will be a pleasure."

The next day, the *Star* reported the meeting. Belva read it to Lura:

"EQUAL RIGHTS MEETING — FEMALE SUFFRAGE. A meeting was held last evening at room no. 11, Washington Building, for the purpose of forming an Equal Rights Association, which was attended by ladies and gentlemen of both colors. Mr. John H. Crane presided, and Mrs. J. A. Archibald acted as secretary. The object of the association is to secure equal rights to all American citizens, without regard to race, color or sex . . ."

Lura said, "I'll read it later, Mother. I have an appointment."

Belva stopped her, "Wait. You know what Mr. Crane said? He said most men oppose female suffrage because it takes away womanhood. But these same men lie in bed and permit their wives to split wood to get breakfast with and think nothing of it." Lura laughed and hurried from the room.

Belva put down the newspaper. She thought about Ezekiel Lockwood. He wasn't the kind of man who would lie in bed while his wife split wood for breakfast. The world needed more men like him.

Belva met Dr. Lockwood at meetings often after the evening at the Washington Building. Eventually the Universal Franchise Association was formed. Senator Pomeroy was elected president and Josephine S.

Griffing, James H. Holmes, John H. Crane and Belva were chosen vice-presidents. Ezekiel Lockwood escorted Belva home after each meeting. Lura teased her mother about her new beau.

"Lura, for heaven's sakes, he's more than twenty years older than I am."

"I don't care, Mother, there's a glow about you I've never seen."

"Speaking about glows, young lady, you've been seeing a lot of DeForest Ormes, haven't you?" Lura blushed. Her mother hugged her, "He seems like a nice young man. I have no objections. As for me, I'm too busy even to think about getting married."

Belva meant what she said. Her life was busy enough. She didn't need marriage. And that's what she told Ezekiel Lockwood when he asked her to marry him. But he wouldn't accept her excuses. He continued to ask her, assuring her that he wouldn't interfere with her work, but she turned down his every proposal. He asked again and again. Finally Belva could refuse no longer. She did love him and wanted to marry him.

On March 11, 1868, Belva Bennett McNall married Ezekiel Lockwood. It was a quiet ceremony. Lura was their only attendant. On the way home in the carriage, Ezekiel reached for Belva's hand and held it. Belva realized how lonely she had been.

Chapter Five

*E*zekiel Lockwood had said he wouldn't interfere with Belva's activities and he didn't. In fact, he told her often how fortunate he was to have married a woman with whom he could have intelligent conversations. The topics discussed in the Lockwood home ranged from the work on the Washington Monument to the impeachment of President Andrew Johnson. And, of course, there was always speculation about which states would ratify the Fourteenth Amendment and which ones wouldn't.

The newspaper stories from around the country were not encouraging. According to the *Revolution*, a newspaper published by Susan B. Anthony and edited by Elizabeth Stanton and Parker Pillsbury, the amendment was gaining in popularity.

Belva doubled her speaking schedule. She wrote more letters. She asked Lura and Ezekiel to write some and, while Belva gave her speeches, Lura and Ezekiel worked together on the letter campaign. But, despite her efforts, the amendment became law. Immediately Belva began to talk about a fifteenth amendment that would take the objectionable word "male" off the record.

When Lura went west to visit her grandparents, Belva taught classes again. She was tired. She thought this activity, added to her already busy schedule, might be the cause of her listlessness. But when an extra hour of sleep each night didn't help, she went to see a doctor. Before he gave her his diagnosis, she knew what it would be. She was going to have a baby.

Now, Ezekiel insisted she give up some of her projects. She didn't argue. She was often exhausted. She had to let something go. She decided on the school. She would close it for a while so she could continue her work for equal rights.

But she did argue when Ezekiel asked her not to go to meetings. "They're too dangerous. You never know what the audience will do."

Belva went to the closet and took out her gray dress.

"I have to go tonight. I want to hear Josephine Griffing give her speech."

Ezekiel protested. "You promised not to interfere, Ezekiel," Belva said.

"That was before you were going to have a child. Now I must insist that you stay home."

Belva put on her dress. They argued. She wouldn't change her mind. Ezekiel took his coat from the closet. "If you won't stay home, I'll go with you. But if there's any trouble, we'll leave."

Belva smiled, "Of course, Ezekiel," she said.

In the hall, Belva sat in the front row with Ezekiel, DeForest Ormes, Lura's beau, and Lura, who had returned from her trip the previous day. The crowd chattered and shuffled their feet. Belva felt the tension. Josephine began her speech. She looked calm, but Belva knew she wasn't. A kettle rolled down the aisle, and a rolling pin. A man's voice jeered, "Get back to the kitchen where you belong." An egg splattered near Josephine's feet. Senator Pomeroy demanded order. A tomato hit him in the face and ran down his whiskers. Several men chanted, "A woman's place is in the home. A woman's place is in the home."

Belva stood up, her face a mask of anger. She rolled back the kettle and threw the rolling pin up the aisle. The men ceased their chant. The laughter stopped, and the crowd grew quiet. Josephine began to speak.

58

Belva sat down and Ezekiel reached for her hand. She tried to stop it from shaking. "We're staying," she whispered to her husband. He didn't make a move to go.

On June 25, a delegation from the Universal Franchise Association went before a House committee to urge the passage of a bill presented in the House of Representatives by the Honorable Henry D. Washburn. The bill contained the coveted words: "Be it enacted . . . that from and after the passage of this act, no person shall be debarred from voting or holding office in the District of Columbia by reason of sex."

Because of another meeting, Belva couldn't appear before the committee. But Josephine Griffing reported to her the next day. "Belva, I wish you could have been with us yesterday," Josephine said after she and Belva had settled down in the parlor. "We conducted our business efficiently and professionally. And the men listened to us. They really listened."

"That's a victory right there," Belva said.

Josephine nodded. "You should have heard Mary Corner. Judge Walker was so interested in what she said, he took notes."

Belva asked, "Did she remind him that men refuse to give us the right to elect officials, but those officials tax us and make our laws?"

"Yes. Then she said that under the law the only

people not allowed to vote are minors, felons, rebels, idiots and aliens. And, since women don't fall into these categories, they should have the right to vote."

"Good for Mary. What did our honorable representatives say to that?" Belva asked.

"Nothing. They just nodded and listened. We were there about an hour, and they gave us their complete attention."

Belva said, "I wonder if they'll ever use those notes."

Josephine said, "Of course they will. I know they will." Belva wasn't as optimistic as her friend, or as trusting. A month later, on July 28, the Fourteenth Amendment became law.

To save rent money, Belva suggested to Ezekiel that he move his dental business from the Washington Building to the Union League Hall. He welcomed the opportunity to spend more time with her. He came to the apartment for lunch or to relax with a cup of tea. However, he found Belva more interested in law books than in conversation.

One afternoon, annoyed by Belva's failure to answer his question about dinner, Ezekiel asked, "Where did this sudden interest in law come from?"

Belva put down her copy of Blackstone's *Commentaries*. "It isn't sudden. I've been interested in law since I took a class during college."

Ezekiel picked up a book and glanced at several pages. "Aren't these difficult to understand?"

"I read passages over and over until I understand them. It keeps my mind occupied during my *confinement*."

Belva emphasized the word confinement. She resented the idea that in the progressive year of 1868, when the battle for equal rights was fought and debated in newspapers, in meeting halls and on street corners, a pregnant woman was still expected not to offend people's sensibilities by appearing in public except on urgent business.

To Belva, the first annual meeting of the Universal Franchise Association was urgent business. On September 25, she not only attended the meeting, she gave a speech. There had been much debate in the Senate about the need for a fifteenth amendment to clarify parts of the Fourteenth Amendment. Belva told her audience there was no need for a fifteenth amendment to clarify the Fourteenth. The only need was for a fifteenth amendment that said all citizens over twenty-one could vote, regardless of sex or race.

Her audience applauded. Several men whistled their approval. Senator George W. Julian was one of them. Later he submitted a proposal to Congress that said the right of suffrage should be based on citizenship without regard to race, color or sex. This was a repetition of Belva's words. She thanked Senator Julian for putting them in the public records.

In January 1869, Susan B. Anthony arrived in Washington for the first woman suffrage meeting held in the Capitol. She brought news of trouble among the members of the Equal Rights Association. She told Belva about it one evening before a meeting.

"Many of our members want us to support a fifteenth amendment that will give the right to vote to Negroes but won't give it to women."

"That's insane," Belva said.

"They say the amendment has a better chance of passing if women are excluded."

"What does Elizabeth Stanton say about it?" Belva asked.

"Elizabeth and I can't support such an amendment."

Belva said, "Nor can I. Women and Negroes have been political outcasts together. They should be given the right to vote together."

"You know, of course, that Elizabeth and I have been asked to resign from the Equal Rights Association because we oppose the amendment, as is?"

"I read it in the *Revolution*. You're not going to do it, are you?"

Susan sighed. She looked tired. "Maybe we can

convince people at the convention that we're right," she said.

But she couldn't. Although there were strong debates to support an amendment that granted votes to both Negroes and women, the convention ended with the proposal that the Fifteenth Amendment make no mention of sex.

A month later, Congress passed it by an overwhelming majority. And in May, Susan and Elizabeth left the Equal Rights Association. With loyal followers, they formed the National Woman Suffrage Association. Its sole purpose was to secure the right of women to vote. Belva applauded their decision.

Belva was bitterly disappointed with the passage of the Fifteenth Amendment, but she wouldn't be kept down. Within days she was talking about a sixteenth amendment. "One of them has to be ours," she told Ezekiel, Lura and anyone else who would listen. She even said it to the midwife the night Jessie Belva Lockwood was born. Later, as the baby lay next to her in bed, Belva told Ezekiel, "This little girl will not be discriminated against. She will enjoy equality with men." Ezekiel took the baby. Belva drifted off to sleep. The words "equality with men" were still with her when she awakened.

One morning several weeks later, Ezekiel came to the apartment with one of his patients. Belva had just put Jessie down for a nap. "This is Dr. Samson, Belva. He's president of Columbian College," Ezekiel said.

"How do you do, Dr. Samson."

The man said, "I've been looking forward to meeting you, Mrs. Lockwood. Your husband has told me of your interest in law. It's highly unusual for a woman."

"Women are interested in many things," Belva said.

"I suppose they are, Mrs. Lockwood," Dr. Samson said, as though such a thing had never occurred to him.

Ezekiel said, "Dr. Samson is giving a series of lectures at the college. He invited us to hear the first one."

Belva smiled, "Thank you, Dr. Samson. That's very kind of you."

"You're welcome, Mrs. Lockwood," Dr. Samson said. He went to the door and opened it. "See you then."

Belva hugged her husband after Dr. Samson had gone. "Thank you, Ezekiel. I know you arranged it."

Ezekiel chuckled. "You wouldn't have been this excited if we had been invited to President Grant's inaugural ball in January," he said.

Lura came in. "Who was invited to the President's ball?"

"Nobody, Lura. Ezekiel is teasing me about a lecture we're going to hear at Columbian College. Dr.

Samson is lecturing on law. Will you stay with Jessie?" Belva asked.

"I hear they have an excellent law course there," Lura told her.

"They do," Belva said.

After Dr. Samson's lecture, Belva talked of little else. When he spoke again, Belva went without Ezekiel and without an invitation. She came home and told her husband, "I'm going to take that law course at Columbian."

"Did Dr. Samson say you could?"

"I didn't talk to Dr. Samson. I decided on the way home."

Ezekiel said, "Belva, that course is for men."

"Who said it's for men?"

"There's no woman in it."

"That doesn't mean it's not open to them. Don't worry. I'll get in," Belva said.

The night of the third lecture, she brought money to pay for the course. When she gave it to the man at the registration desk, he said, "I can't enroll you."

"Why not?" Belva asked impatiently.

"We've never had a woman enroll in our law course," the man said.

"Then it's time you did." Belva put the money in front of him.

"I can't take it, madam. It's not up to me." Belva's

face filled with anger. "I'll submit your request to the faculty, however," the man said quickly.

When Belva got home and told Ezekiel what had happened, she was grateful he didn't say, "I told you so." She couldn't have held her temper.

A week passed and another. Lura told her mother that everything would be all right. Ezekiel agreed with her. Belva appreciated their encouragement, but as the days passed, she felt her chances grow slimmer.

One morning Lura brought the mail to the breakfast table. "Here's one from Columbian College."

Belva reached for the envelope and tore it open. She read the letter aloud:

> Columbian College, Oct. 7, 1869
>
> Mrs. Belva A. Lockwood:
>
> "Madam, The Faculty of Columbian College have considered your request to be admitted to the Law Department of this institution, and after due consultation, have considered that such admission would not be expedient, as it would be likely to distract the attention of the young men.
>
> Respectfully,
>
> GEO. W. SAMSON, PRES."

Belva put down the letter. "Likely to distract the attention of the young men," she said. "I'm not a belle of eighteen. I'm a married woman who will be thirty-nine years old in two weeks."

Her husband and her daughter didn't say anything. Belva sensed their sympathy. Finally Lura said, "It's rather a compliment when you think about it, Mother."

Ezekiel agreed with her. Belva said, "I don't want compliments. I want to take a law course." She crumpled the letter and threw it down. "Is that asking so much?"

Chapter Six

Belva wondered what to do about the letter. It seemed useless to go to Dr. Samson and plead for a chance to prove herself. He would blame the "no woman rule" on the board of trustees, and she knew there was no hope of changing the thinking of that group of men. The easiest thing would be to do nothing, but that was cowardly. Until women let people know of their rejections, they would remain second-class citizens. Without consulting Ezekiel, she called a meeting in the Union League Hall and invited members of the press.

She told her audience that women must stop being afraid. More of them had to speak out against injustice. She ended her speech by saying, "I've been laughed at many times in this hall, I've hated it, but I've endured it for a cause. However, I must confess that because I hate to be laughed at, I've often failed to pursue a goal. But I'm convinced that a better future for women depends on their willingness to make the effort to pull down barriers. If that means being laughed at, then I shall endure it."

A reporter asked, "How do you intend to break those barriers, Mrs. Lockwood?"

Belva said, "I'm going to study law."

Another reporter asked, "Have you registered anywhere?"

"I've applied at Columbian College, but they refused to accept my registration." The reporter asked why and Belva told him, "Because I'm a woman."

She reached in her pocket and pulled out the letter from Dr. Samson. Ezekiel leaped to his feet. "Ladies and gentlemen, the meeting is finished," he said.

The audience became more curious. "What do you have there, Mrs. Lockwood?" a reporter asked.

Ezekiel pulled Belva gently aside. "The interview is finished, gentlemen," he said. The people protested, but Ezekiel dismissed them.

In the apartment Belva asked angrily, "What's the matter with you, Ezekiel? You were rude."

"You were going to show them that letter, weren't you?"

"Yes, I was. Why shouldn't I?"

"Dr. Samson is an elder at our church. I don't think he should have this publicity."

"Why not? He wrote the letter, didn't he?"

"He wrote it because, as president of the college, he had to. It wasn't anything personal."

"Then as president of the college, he should have the publicity," Belva took the letter from her pocket. "It isn't anything personal," she said bitterly.

"Belva, I know how much you wanted this, but showing that letter to the press couldn't help you."

"It would make people aware that women can't take their places in the professions, because they can't take their places in the schools." They argued a long time. They went to bed with the problem unresolved.

Early the next morning Belva found reporters at her door. They wanted to know more about the letter. "Show it to us," one of them said.

"It's in the public interest," another one said.

The others agreed. Belva went to her bedroom. Ezekiel was still asleep. She returned to the reporters and read the letter to them. Ezekiel would be angry, but Belva believed that it was truly in the public interest.

Ezekiel didn't know what Belva had done until he read it in the evening paper. He was furious. She was trying to calm him when Lura came into the kitchen.

70

Her face glowed with excitement. "DeForest wants to ask you something," she said. "He's waiting in the parlor."

The three of them went to the parlor where DeForest sat on the edge of the Morris chair fingering his watch fob. He stood up. He blushed and stammered before he managed to ask, "May I have your daughter's hand in marriage?"

Belva and Ezekiel weren't surprised. Lura had been keeping company with DeForest for months. Still there was much to discuss. By the time they had given the children their blessing, most of Ezekiel's anger at Belva's action had eased. Later when the two of them talked, he was able to joke about it. "I hope DeForest has the minister put emphasis on the word obey in the marriage ceremony," he said.

Belva laughed. "Ezekiel, you know that word shouldn't even be in the marriage vows."

"You'll have trouble convincing men of that. Women too for that matter."

"I'll leave that to others. For the moment I'll have enough to do answering questions about that newspaper story."

However, there was little interest in an article about a woman who had been turned away from a law course. Still, several requests for speeches came in as interest grew. Belva tried to register at schools that

71

offered law courses. The registrar always turned her down. She gave more speeches. She discussed the problem with congressmen. Between appointments she helped Lura with her wedding preparations. They planned a religious ceremony and, when the minister asked Lura if she promised to love, honor and obey, Ezekiel nudged Belva. She smiled. "It's traditional," she whispered.

With Jessie and DeForest added to the family, the Lockwoods enjoyed a happy Christmas. Jessie was the center of attention. She laughed at her jack-in-the-box, she poked the eyes of a doll larger than she was, and she squealed when Belva pulled her around the parlor in a new red wagon. When the wagon stopped, Jessie reached for a gingerbread man on the Christmas tree. Ezekiel moved her away. Belva said, "Let her, Ezekiel. Christmas is for children." She looked at Lura and back at Jessie. "And they're children for so little time," she said.

After the new year, Belva learned about a bill Mr. Arnell of Tennessee had introduced in Congress. It would give employees who worked for the government equal pay for equal work, regardless of sex. And if women did more important work than men, the women would receive more money. Belva made an appointment to talk to him.

When they met in his office she said, "Mr. Arnell, I want to thank you for introducing your bill."

Mr. Arnell smiled. "I feel it's the most important bill I've ever introduced. It will restore dignity to thousands of women." He leaned forward in his chair. "One of my neighbors died several months ago, and his widow isn't able to support her children on the starvation wages the government pays her. She has to beg help from friends, yet she works beside men who earn twice as much as she does."

"That doesn't happen only in government jobs," Belva said. "Wouldn't it be wiser to pass a bill that would guarantee equal pay in private industry also?"

"That was my first idea. But I felt if I put in a clause like that, the bill would be defeated in committee. It's better to set a precedent and go from there than ask for so much that I get nothing."

Belva asked, "What is the chance of its passing?"

"It will depend on how many people let their congressmen know they want it passed. I have several people out getting signatures on petitions right now," Mr. Arnell picked up a sheet of paper and gave it to Belva. She read the words "equal pay for equal work."

"Can you use more help?" she asked.

Mr. Arnell rose. "We can always use more help, Mrs. Lockwood." Belva left the office with several petitions.

She went to her friends. She learned many of them were already working for the bill. Mary Corner said, "We need workers in other cities. I'd like to go to New York, but I can't get away. Do you know if anyone is going to the convention this year?"

Belva said, "I wasn't going, but there's no reason why I shouldn't. I could attend the meetings and get signatures at the same time."

"Who will stay with Jessie?" Mary asked.

"Ezekiel can take care of her. He's always looking for an excuse to get me out of the house so he can spoil her."

Mary laughed, "I can understand how easy that would be. She's a beautiful child."

Belva didn't wait until she arrived in New York to get signatures on her petition. She asked everyone on the train if they would sign it. Few people did. They didn't agree that a woman should get paid the same salary as a man. But things were different in New York. At least they were different at the meetings where people understood the need for Mr. Arnell's bill. When Belva returned home, she had hundreds of names to add to the congressman's list.

When the bill passed with the words, ". . . that, in the employment of labor, clerical or other, in any branch of the civil service of the United States, no discrimination shall be made in favor of either sex,"

Belva remembered the day she had sat in widow's black before the school trustees in Royalton and was offered half the pay that male teachers received.

One morning after Belva had put Jessie down for her nap, a man came to the apartment. He introduced himself as Professor William Wedgewood. He told Belva, "Mrs. Lockwood, I read about Columbian College's refusal to admit you. I think it's unfortunate."

Belva said, "I won't argue that point, Professor Wedgewood." She sat down and gestured to the chair across from her. "May I ask why you're here?"

"When I read about your rejection at Columbian I wanted to help you, but there wasn't anything I could do at the time. Now there is. I plan to open a school this fall — the National University Law School — and I've come to ask you to join the classes."

For a moment Belva wondered if she had heard correctly. When she decided she had, she thought the offer might be a way of getting publicity for the new school. She asked, "As the only woman?"

Professor Wedgewood said, "Oh, no, my offer will go out to all women who want to join." They talked about the curriculum. "Will you apply?" Professor Wedgewood asked.

"You can be certain of it," Belva said.

The moment Professor Wedgewood left, Belva ran to Ezekiel's office. "Ezekiel, it's happened."

Her husband looked up from the patient in the dental chair. Both men were obviously annoyed at the interruption. "Belva, can't you see I'm busy?"

Belva ignored his question. "I'm going to study law."

Ezekiel stopped working. The patient grumbled. He pointed to his mouth. Ezekiel got back to work. He said to Belva, "Tell me. Where? When?"

With little attention to the patient's complaints about the intrusion, Belva told her husband of Professor Wedgewood's visit. When Ezekiel finished, the patient left, grumbling about the pain and the lack of sympathy.

Belva and Ezekiel went to the apartment. He asked, "Who will stay with Jessie? I can't always be ready to take care of her needs. Patients walk in at all hours."

Belva agreed. It was one thing to care for the baby for a week while Belva went to New York, but it was something else to take care of her every day while Belva went to school. They discussed the problem until another patient came, but they found no solution. However, that evening when Lura and DeForest came to visit, Lura settled the problem.

"I'll take care of her, Mother. You know I'd love to," she said. Belva hugged her. At thirty-nine she was free to go to college.

As summer passed — a blistering Washington summer — Belva became more and more anxious to get started with her studies. If it hadn't been for Jessie, time would have dragged endlessly. The child was intelligent and curious. She seldom walked. Instead she ran around the house feeling, tasting and smelling everything she came in contact with. It made Belva happy just to be with her.

One morning Jessie awoke with tears instead of a smile. Belva picked her up. Jessie pressed close to her. Belva felt her forehead. It was hot. She carried her to the kitchen. "Jessie has a fever," she told Ezekiel.

Ezekiel said, "It's probably from this heat. I couldn't sleep last night, it was so hot."

Belva pushed back Jessie's blond hair. She felt her head again. "It's more than the heat, she's burning up. You'd better go for the doctor."

The doctor came around ten. Jessie was asleep. She moaned while he examined her. He looked at Belva and Ezekiel. "It's the fever," he said.

"Typhoid?" Belva asked. He nodded. "That means she's going to . . . she's going to die?"

"She's a strong child, Mrs. Lockwood. She may be able to fight it." Jessie moaned. Perspiration soaked her bed. "We have to get that fever down," the doctor said. "Fix a tub of cold water to put her in."

Ezekiel ran to fill the metal tub while Belva took off Jessie's nightgown. She carried her to the bath and eased her in. The little girl cried. Belva started to take her out. "Leave her, it will lower the fever," the doctor said. Jessie continued to cry. Belva longed to hold her, but she followed the doctor's orders. Before he left, the child was back in her crib sleeping quietly, her fever almost gone.

But it returned. It returned with an intensity that frightened Belva. She ran to Ezekiel's office. He went back to the apartment with her. They repeated the cold bath. They sat and waited. For days they scarcely slept. Lura and DeForest joined the vigil. They worried and prayed, but all their love and attention couldn't save Jessie. While her family surrounded her bed, she died in her sleep. She was only eighteen months old.

At first Belva refused to accept the loss, but finally she had to. Jessie was no longer there to play with, to talk to, to hug. The summer had seemed endless. Now each day had no end; and the nights . . . Belva hated the nights because they came before mornings — mornings that would be empty without Jessie.

Ezekiel, Lura and DeForest joined together to help Belva. She scarcely heard them. One day at breakfast Ezekiel said, "Don't you have things to prepare for school? A woman can't go to college without the latest in fashion." Belva stared at him. "I'm sorry. I shouldn't have said that. But, Belva, I don't know what to say. Jessie's loss is my loss too. And I've not only lost her, I've lost you. We've all lost you." He put his arms around her.

Belva's eyes filled with tears. "I'm sorry, Ezekiel. You've all been wonderful, and I've been selfish." She pulled away from him. "But I can't go to school now."

"Of course you can. You need activity. Without it, you'll become lost in your grief."

Belva knew he was right. When classes started she went. For moments at school she pushed aside her grief. But when she went home, the house was empty. The grief returned.

Chapter Seven

*B*elva *was disappointed* that only fifteen women took advantage of Professor Wedgewood's offer to study law. She was more disappointed when some of the women dropped out of the course before the end of the first semester. One woman said there was too much abuse from the men. Another said the lessons were too difficult. And one left because, "Men aren't interested in women who show too much intelligence."

Belva hated to see them go. Their decision gave people one more reason to say that women were quitters. And one of the male students wasted no time in asking her when she would leave.

Belva fought the urge to hit him with her umbrella. "Sir, I shall not quit. The men may insult me. They may keep me from giving recitations in class. They may add more pressure. But they will never make me quit." She tightened her grip on the umbrella. "Never," she said.

The man sauntered away. "We'll see," he called back.

One morning Belva was on her way to the lecture room when Lydia Hall stopped her. "There's no need to go," she said, her voice angry and low.

"It's almost nine o'clock. "We'll be late," Belva said.

"Women have been barred from the lectures."

Belva stared at her. "Why?"

The men students don't want us," Lydia said.

"That's ridiculous!"

"I've just come from the hall. They sent me away."

"I'm going to talk to Professor Wedgewood," Belva said. She ran up the path to the lecture hall. She was back with Lydia almost immediately. "I couldn't see him. He's lecturing," she said.

Belva and Lydia went to their next class. The men didn't talk to them, but Belva didn't care. As long as she could continue the course, she would tolerate anything.

That afternoon she went to see Professor Wedgewood. "Why are women restricted from lectures?" she asked angrily.

"The men threatened to walk out if women continue to attend lectures. They say their presence disturbs them."

"You're going to let them dictate to you?" Belva asked.

"Mrs. Lockwood, try to understand my position," Professor Wedgewood pleaded. "If the men leave, I'll have to close the school. That would solve nothing."

Belva bit her lip in anger. "How about the classes?" she asked.

"You may go on with regular classes. Of course, women will continue to give their recitations the way they have been doing — after the men have left the room."

"I thought women would have equal opportunities in your school," Belva said.

"Prejudice dies hard, Mrs. Lockwood. When I opened the school I hoped things would be different."

"I hoped they would be too," Belva said. She went to the door.

Professor Wedgewood asked. "You won't quit, will you?" Belva felt he wanted her to stay.

"Not until I get my degree, Professor Wedgewood." She saw his smile before she closed the door.

She walked out into the biting cold. Something wet hit her cheek. She looked at the sky — a snowflake. A woman walked toward her, and the silvery-wrapped packages she carried reminded Belva it would soon be Christmas. She thought of the red wagon, the laughing child. There would be no tree at the Lockwoods' this year, no gingerbread man, no Jessie. Belva pulled her cape tightly around her and walked slowly home.

Shortly after the school's Christmas holiday, two more women dropped Professor Wedgewood's course. Belva told Ezekiel that evening, "There's only five of us left. And I'm afraid the others will leave before long too."

"Did they leave because of the men's insults?" Ezekiel asked.

Belva nodded. "And they felt cheated. The men take part in make-believe trials. They learn by doing. We women aren't allowed to do anything, but sit and listen. We can't argue a point. We can't make suggestions. It's maddening."

Ezekiel said, "But you've learned other things. You know how to complete legal forms, and you know how to write a will."

Belva said, "Yes, and I've learned a lawyer's first duty is to his client." Her voice flowed with sarcasm. "It will be helpful if I ever have a client."

Ezekiel said, "You'll have clients. People are paying a lot of attention to women in law schools. Just the other day Judge Cartter asked the courts not to talk about lawyers as males. He said now that there are women in law school, there would soon be women practicing law and the group should be called attorneys with no mention of sex."

Belva said, "I know. I've wanted to write and thank him." She stretched. "I'll do it in the morning. I'm going to bed. Susan should be here in a few days for the woman's suffrage convention, and I want to be well rested for the meetings."

In her room Belva took the pins from her curls and let them fall to her shoulders. While she brushed her hair, she prayed the other women students would not leave school.

When Susan arrived in Washington, Belva was shocked at the way many of the delegates treated the woman who had traveled around the country usually at her own expense to ask equal rights for women. But Susan still had many followers and they went together to hear Victoria Woodhull give a speech. Belva had read many newspaper stories about the stockbroker from New York. Dissatisfied with the way her male coworkers treated her, Victoria had opened her own brokerage house. The press called her the flamboyant stockbroker.

Dressed in a red velvet coat, a plumed hat over her well-coiffed hair, she lived up to her title. Belva listened to her repeat the words so many women had said before audiences, before committees, before anyone who would listen: all persons born or naturalized in the United States were citizens of the United States, and all citizens over twenty-one had the right to vote.

When Victoria finished, Susan asked to speak. To Belva's surprise, the committee gave her permission. In her gray woolen dress, Susan was a startling contrast to Victoria's elegance, but her message was the same. Women were entitled to vote. Before she finished, Susan told the men they would have to make a decision on what she and Victoria had said, because one day a woman would test the legality of the amendment by going to the polls to cast a ballot.

Outside, Belva told Susan, "Someone should put that amendment to a test at the next presidential election."

Susan gave her a sly look. "Maybe someone will," she said.

Belva would have liked to discuss the matter in class. It would have been interesting to get a man's opinion on an amendment that helped keep women second-class citizens. But she stayed silent. So did the other female students.

As the months passed, the men stepped up their campaign to get rid of the women. The insults became more frequent. The men continued to keep women out of the lecture halls. They refused to let them take part in the hypothetical cases Professor Wedgewood presented. While male students questioned fictitious witnesses, addressed juries and worked out legal maneuvers, the women sat silent, ignored and barred from uttering a word. Two more quit. When classes ended in June only three women remained, and the men made it clear that if these three returned in September, they would soon be driven out.

Belva took advantage of her vacation to make friends with lawyers trying real cases in the courts of Washington and to organize a march to the voting registrar's office. More than seventy women took part in the demonstration. They carried banners and chanted: "We want to vote. We want to vote." When the women reached the registrar's office they told him, "We are American citizens, and as citizens we demand the right to vote under the Fourteenth Amendment of the Constitution." The registrar asked them to leave. The protestors repeated their demand. He threatened to call the militia, but the women stayed. A crowd gathered. A man said to Belva, "If I were your husband, I would lock you up."

Belva declared, "Sir, you could never be my husband."

The women asked for support. After the crowd had listened to their request, many promised to help. The marchers thanked them and dispersed without the use of the militia.

After Lura read about the incident, she told Belva, "Mother, sometimes I think all you want out of life is the right to cast a ballot."

Belva looked at her daughter. Lura would be a mother herself soon. "I fight for the ballot because we can do little until we have our say in the government. And I'll wager when we get it, we'll do better than men have done. They elected Grant, and now they complain he's the worst President they've ever had."

Lura said, "They said that about Andrew Johnson too. In fact they probably have said that about every President they've elected."

Belva laughed. "That's what I mean," she said.

Lura stood up. "I have to go. I have an appointment with my doctor."

"When can I expect my grandchild?" Belva asked.

"The doctor said in about three weeks."

"That means I'll be a grandmother when I return to college."

"Perhaps," Lura said.

Belva thought about it. "I wonder if that will impress those brash men students," she said. The baby was born shortly before school started, but there was no special consideration for a grandmother.

Soon after classes resumed, another woman quit the course. "I can't take the men's insults any longer," the woman said. "And I've wasted too much time already.

Even if we graduate, we won't be able to try a case. The men won't let us."

Belva told her, "People are working for us. Judge Cartter got the laws of the district revised. And I've met lawyers who have promised to give us a chance. Don't quit now."

The woman wouldn't listen. She left Belva and Lydia Hall alone. A week later they received letters that stated they could continue classes, but they would not get diplomas when they finished in May.

Belva stormed into Professor Wedgewood's office. She waved the letter in front of his face. "What is the meaning of this?"

"Mrs. Lockwood, lower your voice, please," Professor Wedgewood said. He rolled his chair from his desk and away from her. "There's nothing I can do."

Belva leaned over the desk. "What do you mean there's nothing you can do? It's your school isn't it?" Her voice resounded through the office.

"Mrs. Lockwood, please. It's my school, but I must go with the majority. The men said they wouldn't sit on a stage with women, nor would they let their names appear on a list of graduates that contained women's names. They threatened to walk out. This school is my only source of income."

"That 'they threatened to walk out' phrase was believable when the course began, but you don't think these men are foolish enough to walk out when they're almost finished."

Professor Wedgewood shrugged. "The majority rules, Mrs. Lockwood."

Belva threw the letter on his desk. "You men will always have the majority," she said and stomped out of the room.

Belva's outburst did her no good. When the graduating class of the National University Law School received their diplomas in May 1872, Belva and Lydia Hall were not on stage. Their names were not on the program. It was as though they hadn't attended the school at all.

Despite the snub, Belva and Lydia applied for admission to the District of Columbia Supreme Court. It turned them down. The Washington *Star* recorded the event while the *Chronicle* mistakenly reported that the women were members of the bar. Belva read the short notice to Ezekiel at breakfast, "And now a woman takes her place as attorney at our District Bar. A petticoated lawyer! What would the ante-bellum city of Washington have said could it have known?" Belva put down the paper. "It would have said nothing. Their precious man's world is still safe."

Ezekiel said, "You have the knowledge; nobody can take that from you. You can work in a law office and fill out legal papers. You've passed the college finals. You're a lawyer in every sense of the word."

"In every sense but one. I can't practice law in the courts."

But Belva wouldn't accept defeat. After lunch she combed her hair into curls at the sides of her head and pulled the rest of her hair into a knot at the nape of her neck. She put on her blue velvet suit, pinned a hat over her curls, picked up her parasol and rode the horsecar to the college. Professor Wedgewood received her cordially. Belva sat across from him poised and serene. Her outbursts had produced no results. She would try charm.

"Professor, now that the men have received their diplomas and have gone their separate ways, what harm can it do to give Lydia and me our diplomas?" she asked.

"No harm, Mrs. Lockwood. As a matter of fact I met with the faculty yesterday to ask them to sign the diplomas. They refused." Professor Wedgewood moved uncomfortably in his chair. Belva wondered if he were telling the truth. "Several of them were willing to put their names to the document, but others balked. Also there's another problem. President Grant would have to sign the diploma. He's not only the President of the United States, he's also president of the National University Law School. I fear we'd have a difficult time getting his signature."

Belva knew that President Grant was connected with the school. His name was printed on all its correspondence, but she had no idea he would have to sign her diploma. "Why don't you ask him? He may surprise you and do it."

"Mrs. Lockwood, please be sensible. The President is much too busy to be bothered with things like this. Let me meet with the faculty again. We may be able to work something out."

Belva went to see Professor Wedgewood every day. Every day he asked for more time. After a few weeks, she asked for only one diploma. Lydia Hall had married and left the area.

One morning Belva didn't go talk to Professor Wedgewood. Instead, she went to see Francis Miller, a friend of the women's rights movement and a distinguished member of the bar.

"Mr. Miller, will you move for my admission to the bar of the Supreme Court of the District of Columbia?" she asked him.

"Did you get your diploma?" Mr. Miller said.

"No, I didn't. That's why I came to you. I'm going to change my strategy. Will you try to obtain permission for me to take the examinations that will admit me to the court?"

Mr. Miller puffed his cigar. He offered no words of encouragement. Belva waited. "I'll do what I can, Mrs. Lockwood," Mr. Miller said. "But I can promise nothing. These things come slowly even under the best circumstances."

"I understand. I'll be patient," Belva said.

While she waited, Belva spent most of her time in the courts. Weeks passed. She made friends with lawyers and judges. She learned the first names of the law clerks and court officials. She saw them almost daily. Someone, somewhere, would let her practice law.

It was late July before Belva and Francis Miller had convinced people to give her a chance. She went before a committee to take her examination. The first day she came home exhausted and told Ezekiel she had to go back. The next day she told him, "I think they've asked me about every precedent in the books. I wouldn't be surprised if they go back as far as the Bible tomorrow."

"You have to go back tomorrow?" Ezekiel asked. Belva nodded. He said, "How do you think you're doing?"

"I'm holding my own. And they know I'm holding my own. I think that's why the examination is so long and difficult."

"You'll pass," Ezekiel said confidently.

Belva sighed, "It may not matter. The committee has to approve my admission, and they aren't friendly."

"Won't they have to admit you if you pass?"

Belva put her feet up on the ottoman and rubbed the back of her neck. "They should have to, but I don't know if they will."

After the examination, Belva waited for the committee's report. She spent a lot of time in court. She visited friends. She went to Lura's house and spoiled her granddaughter. Weeks passed. She heard nothing from the committee nor could she get permission to see any of its members. Angry, she entered a complaint with Judge Cartter. He asked the group for its report. The men wouldn't give it. Infuriated, Judge Cartter appointed another committee.

Belva had to take the tests again. When she finished, the new committee also refused to give its report. Belva was back where she started.

On the verge of tears, Lura asked, "Why, Mother? Why won't they tell you how you did?"

Belva said, "I must have passed both sets of tests. As long as the men don't give their report, they don't have to admit that a woman is qualified to practice in the Supreme Court of the nation's capital, but isn't allowed to because of her sex."

Lura said, "They shouldn't get away with that."

"They won't," Belva said.

Chapter Eight

Although her struggle to win acceptance in the courts took much of Belva's energy, she still found strength to work for Horace Greeley, the Democratic nominee for the Presidency. She wasn't convinced of his ability to do the job, but she believed one term of the scandal-ridden Grant administration was enough. She didn't have a vote, but she had a voice. She went on the campaign trail. She traveled by train, by horse and by coach. Often she rode all night to reach the next town before morning. She slept in bug-infested beds. She missed meals. She spoke anywhere a crowd would gather. She felt their response. On the platform in small towns, Belva believed Greeley could win the election. But when she returned to Washington, she learned his chances of winning were slim. She made speeches throughout Washington and the surrounding cities. Grant must be defeated. Every night she fell into bed exhausted.

One morning Lura came to visit with the baby. She asked Belva, "Have you seen the *National Republican*?"

"Not yet. I slept late."

"Susan B. Anthony and a group of women registered to vote in Rochester, New York," Lura said.

Belva smiled. "So she did it."

"What do you mean?"

"Susan said she might test the Fourteenth Amendment in this election," Belva explained. She picked up her grandchild and sat with her in front of the fireplace. "Was there any trouble?" Belva asked Lura.

"The paper doesn't report any. The story says that when the registrar wouldn't give the women registration forms, Miss Anthony read the beginning of the Fourteenth Amendment, and he let them fill out the papers."

Belva admired Susan's action, but she worried about what might happen to Susan if she actually cast a ballot. "I wish her good fortune," Belva said.

Victoria Woodhull took part in politics in a different way than Susan. Victoria announced to the press that she was a candidate for the Presidency. No one took her seriously, and eventually she let the matter drop. Belva was sorry to see Victoria quit. There was no hope of her winning, of course, but it would have made people more aware of the discrimination against women.

On November 5 Belva went with Ezekiel to cast his vote for Horace Greeley. The ballot was only a piece of paper dropped into a wooden box with a slot at the top, but what power it held. She envied Ezekiel his privilege.

As the voting results came in from other parts of the country, Belva knew her candidate had lost. "I'm not certain this country can abide another four years of Ulysses S. Grant," she told Ezekiel.

"The American people have spoken, Belva. We must accept the decision," he said.

"*Half* of the American people have spoken. The other half is supposed to stay home with the pots and pans." She banged the kettle she had just used to boil water. "All except Susan. Susan no longer belongs to the half with the pots and pans. I wonder how she did at the polls."

Several days later, newspapers carried the story. Susan B. Anthony had cast a ballot in the election. "Let's celebrate, Ezekiel," Belva said after she read the story.

Ezekiel put tobacco in his pipe. "Don't you think

we should wait to see if there's anything to celebrate?"

"What do you mean?"

"You're the one who has studied law. Don't you think Susan has broken the law?"

"Of course she hasn't. The Fourteenth Amendment states that all people born in the United States are citizens. Susan was born in Massachusetts. That gives her the right to vote. It's the country that has broken the law, not Susan."

Ezekiel said, "That's a good argument. If there's any trouble, you can use it to defend her."

"How can I defend her? I can't even speak in court." Belva picked up her newspaper and read the story again. No one would harm Susan. Or would they?

Belva advertised for clients. She wrote wills, filled out legal papers and continued her struggles with the courts. Many judges told her they would let her try cases in court if she had a diploma — a piece of paper that would give her no more knowledge of law than she already possessed, but they insisted she needed it.

"I'll be a hundred years old before I can go to court," Belva told Ezekiel after a frustrating day of visits to the courts and arguments with the men who controlled them.

"Why don't you try to get a diploma from another college?" Ezekiel asked.

"That's ridiculous. I've already earned a diploma."

"But you don't have it. And you obviously need one."

Belva tensed with anger. Ezekiel said nothing. She relaxed. It wasn't his fault. "I'll think about it," she said.

Several days later she went to a lecture at Georgetown College. She found it stimulating. She went to another. When it finished, she tried to enroll. The registrar wouldn't take her money. Two days later she received a note from the chancellor. She could no longer attend the lectures. It was a repetition of her experience at Columbian College.

That day Belva met Judge William Snell outside the police court. She told him what happened.

"You don't need a diploma, Mrs. Lockwood. You may practice in my court any time you want," the judge told her.

"Thank you, Judge Snell, but it wouldn't be fair to a client to take his case then have to turn it over to another lawyer if it has to be carried to a higher court."

"It does delay a client's case if a new lawyer has to prepare for it, but try it. You'll gain experience and maybe one of my colleagues in the higher courts will give you a chance."

Belva put her hand on his arm. "Thank you, Judge Snell. We need more men like you."

"We need more women like you, Mrs. Lockwood," the Judge told her.

As a result of the conversation, Belva accepted several clients. Pleased by their trust in her, she spent hours on simple traffic cases. She won them all. But within weeks, one had to be carried to a higher court, and she couldn't take it there. She had to turn her client over to another lawyer, a lawyer who could go on — a man, of course.

Desperate for a diploma that might let her practice in the Supreme Court of the District, Belva registered at Howard University and was accepted. Every day she waited for a letter that would tell her there had been a mistake, but it didn't come. She attended unmolested.

She left for school every morning certain nothing could interfere with her happiness. But one day two items in the newspaper shocked her. Horace Greeley had died November 29, and Susan B. Anthony had been arrested Thanksgiving Day for illegally casting a ballot during the presidential election.

Greeley's death saddened Belva, but Susan's plight filled her thoughts. Belva wrote to Susan to offer help. Every day Belva searched the papers for news of the arrest and ran to the door at the sound of the postman's whistle.

She received no answer to her letter, nor was there

more news in the paper. She imagined Susan in jail, unable to communicate with the outside world. However, in January, Susan arrived for the annual suffrage convention. She was weary, but ready to take her place on the platform. Belva hugged her. "Susan, we thought you were rotting in jail."

Susan laughed. "Belva, it's not as bad as that."

"What happened? Are you free?" Belva asked.

"I'm out on bail."

"When is the trial?" Belva asked.

"In May," Susan said. The delegates milled around. "I have to make the first speech," Susan said. "I'd better get on stage."

After the meeting officially opened, Susan stood to speak. The audience cheered. She tried to shush them. They cheered louder. Susan waited. The noise subsided and she said, "I stand here under indictment for having exercised my right as a citizen to vote at the last election; and by a fiction of the law, I am now in custody and not a free person on this platform." Belva watched the tall, slim woman. She had traveled a long way from the unsure, frightened person Belva had met in New York. Susan held her audience spellbound.

Later in the day Belva made a speech. She told her audience that women had the right to vote under the Constitution, then she read a resolution she had composed.

"To the Honorable Senate and House of Representatives in Congress Assembled:
Resolved: That we, the officers and members of
the National Suffrage Association, in convention
assembled, respectfully ask Congress to enact
appropriate legislation, during its present session,
to protect women citizens in the several States of
this Union in their right to vote."

After the meeting, Ezekiel asked her, "How can you
argue women have the right to vote under the
Constitution, then read a resolution that asks Congress
to pass appropriate legislation to guarantee that right?"

"I'm protecting us from both sides," she said. "If
Congress won't go along with the first lines of the
Fourteenth Amendment, then I've already asked them
to pass laws that will give women their rights."

"You're very thorough," Ezekiel said.

"I'm capable too. And I could prove it, if men
would let me."

"Maybe that's why they don't. Men don't like to
think women are more capable than they are."

"Not all women are more capable than men, just as
not all men are more capable than women. It's the
individual who counts," Belva said.

"Why don't you forget the courts?" Ezekiel asked.
"You don't need them. Your appointment calendar is
almost full. At the rate you're going you'll make as

much money as I will this year just writing wills and deeds and things like that."

"I don't want to just write wills and deeds and things like that. I want to be a trial attorney."

Ezekiel said, "I'm sorry if I've made you angry, Belva. But sometimes it's difficult for me to understand." He put his arm around her. "Do anything you want to become what you want. I'll be with you all the way," he said.

"Thank you, Ezekiel," Belva said, grateful for his support.

Susan's trial was set for May. The papers carried hardly anything about it. When they did, it was to inform readers that the trial had been postponed until June. Belva worried about Susan. The maximum penalty for her "crime" was a five-hundred-dollar fine, three years in jail, or both. Belva called a meeting to consider what the group would do if Susan were convicted. They vowed that if Susan B. Anthony went to jail again, there would be an uproar such as no one had ever heard.

The trial began on a scorching June day. Three days later, the judge found Susan guilty and fined her a hundred dollars. Belva knew that because of Susan's constant traveling and her generosity to the cause, she was always on the verge of poverty. Belva sent her friend money to help pay the fine and promised she would never stop trying for her place in court so she could fight injustices such as the one Susan had endured.

Through the summer, Belva's moods wavered between discouragement and anger. When time came to go back to Howard University, she was thoroughly dissatisfied and furious with herself. She was forty-three years old, a grandmother, and she was still going to school. She had earned a diploma. Why did she have to try for another one? On registration day, instead of going to Howard University, she went to see Professor Wedgewood. The man received her with the familiar story that the faculty refused to sign her diploma.

Belva sat on the edge of the chair across from him. She clenched her parasol. "I've earned that diploma, Professor, and I want it."

"Mrs. Lockwood, it's no use. We're wasting our time." The man shifted his position. "Besides, you don't need a diploma. Many of the lawyers practicing now have never received a degree from a law school. They started as law clerks and worked their way up. Our late President, Mr. Lincoln, started in just that way."

"Abraham Lincoln was a man. And that's what makes the difference," Belva said.

Professor Wedgewood shrugged. "You must be patient."

"I have been patient. And I refuse to be patient any longer." Belva tapped the parasol on the floor and rose. Her voile dress swirled around her as she turned toward the door. She slammed it.

Belva's anger didn't diminish during the ride home. When she reached her front stoop, she ran up the stairs to the apartment. She threw her parasol and hat on a chair. She pulled off her gloves and dropped them on a table on the way to her desk. She sat down and wrote:

> No. 432 Ninth Street, N.W.
> Washington, D.C.
> September 3, 1873

To His Excellency U. S. Grant, President U.S.A.

Sir — You are, or you are not, President of the National University Law School. If you are its president, I desire to say to you that I have passed through the curriculum of study in this school, and am entitled to, and demand my diploma. If you are not its president, then I ask that you take your name from its papers, and not hold out to the world to be what you are not.

> Very respectfully,
> Belva A. Lockwood.

Belva folded the paper and stuffed it into an envelope. She put on her hat, picked up her gloves and parasol and hurried to the post office.

Chapter Nine

When Belva told Ezekiel about her letter to President Grant, her husband whistled. "You believe in going to the top, don't you?" he said.

"I should have done it months ago," Belva said.

"Do you think it will work?"

"If it doesn't, at least I'll know I've done all I can."

A week after Belva had written the letter, Professor Wedgewood came to see her. He handed her a paper. It was her diploma bearing his signature, the signatures of his staff and the signature of the President of the United States. Belva shivered with excitement.

"I wish things could have been different," the red-faced man said and almost ran to the stairs.

"I do too," Belva told the retreating man.

She ran to Ezekiel's office. "I have it! I have it!" She explained about Professor Wedgewood's visit.

Ezekiel hugged her. "What will you do now?"

"I'll go see all those lawyers and judges who said they would help me, if I had a law degree."

Ezekiel embraced her again. She went back to the apartment for her hat and gloves; and, armed with her diploma, went from one office to another. Many men told her they couldn't do anything for her. Belva realized they had said they would help only because they thought they would never have to keep the promise. She held her temper and went on. Eventually she found a number of men who had meant what they said. On September 24, 1873, twenty-one days after she had written her letter to President Grant, Belva was admitted to the bar of the Supreme Court of the District of Columbia.

People crowded around her and Ezekiel. The clerk said, "You went through easily today, Mrs. Lockwood. The world moves in our day. Welcome."

Belva thanked him. The press asked how she felt. "You would have to be a woman to understand," Belva said. She looked around their group. "Since there are no women among you, your readers will never know."

"Women couldn't do this job," a reporter said.

Belva asked him, "Have you given them a chance?"

Justice Arthur McArthur said to Belva, "Bring on as

many woman lawyers as you choose, Mrs. Lockwood. I don't believe they will be a success."

"I wouldn't be too certain of that, Judge. A precedent has been set now."

Judge Cartter came toward her. He said, "Madame, if you come into this court, you will be treated like a man."

Belva said, "Judge Cartter, nothing would compliment me more." The crowd laughed. Belva reached for Ezekiel's hand. They walked home together.

The day after Belva's admittance to the bar, a woman came to see her. She entered the room Belva used as an office at the Union League Hall and stood silent before her.

"May I help you?" Belva asked.

The woman's face was swollen. She had a black eye. "I'm Mary Ann Folker. I want to talk to you about a . . . I want to talk to you about a . . . divorce."

Belva helped the woman to a chair. Between sobs, she told a story of beatings, drunkenness and desertion by her husband.

"Do you know where your husband is now?" Belva asked the crying woman.

"He's at home drunk. He came back two days ago. The children are hungry. They don't have clothes to go to school. I can't get a job. Isn't there some way we can make my husband take care of them?"

Belva leaned against her desk. "Mrs. Folker, if your husband is home, we can't get a divorce decree because of desertion. However, we should be able to get support for the children." Belva took a pad and pencil from her desk to make notes. "How long have the beatings and drunkenness been going on?" she asked.

Mrs. Folker twisted her handkerchief. "Ten years. Almost from the day we got married," she said.

"Ten years! Mrs. Folker, why didn't you see an attorney before this?"

"I did, but he said, 'Madam, it's a woman's job to keep a man happy. Perhaps you haven't done the job well. Go home and try.'" Belva shook her head in disbelief. She wondered how many women suffered this way.

After she questioned her client, Belva told her she would talk to Mr. Folker. A short visit convinced Belva that Mrs. Folker and her children had to be protected. She filed the divorce papers on September 29.

The day of the hearing of *Folker* v. *Folker* the press, the judges, the lawyers and the spectators waited to see how she would handle the case. Belva was scared. She couldn't afford a mistake. When the judge asked for the first witness, she hesitated. Her palms were damp. Her stomach hurt. But her voice was steady when she called one of the Folkers' neighbors to the stand.

The answers to her questions left no doubt that Frederick Folker beat his wife — frequently. Another witness took the stand. Belva became more confident. The witness testified she had seen the plaintiff's husband stagger down their street on many occasions. She said she felt sorry for the children, especially now that the cold weather was coming on. They had little to wear.

When all the witnesses had been called and testimony given, the judge conferred with the attorneys. When he finished, he granted Mrs. Folker a divorce decree, alimony and attorney's fees. Frederick Folker jumped to his feet. "I won't pay it, Your Honor. There's no way you can make me pay."

Mrs. Folker started to cry. The judge called Belva to the bench. "He's a stubborn one, Mrs. Lockwood. I don't think we'll get a penny out of him."

Belva's temper flared at this typical male reaction. "We'll see about that, Your Honor," she said.

The next day she obtained a writ demanding payment. When he still refused to pay the alimony, Frederick Folker went to prison. Within a week, he promised to support his wife and children. Belva had won.

As the weeks passed, many people came to her. They came out of curiosity. They came out of need. They came, as they said, to give her a chance.

The work brought Belva happiness. But Ezekiel worried her. He was often tired. Some days he didn't get out of bed. She nursed him through his colds and respiratory problems. Work piled up, and she hired Lura to help her with the paper work.

Despite the heavy schedule, Belva continued her court appearances. She won many cases, but she knew to be more effective, she would have to specialize. However, she couldn't decide what kind of cases she wanted to devote her life to. She tried everything. She even took an unpopular murder case in which a woman was accused of shooting a constable. The woman insisted she was innocent, and Belva believed her.

When the case went to court, Belva put her client on the stand. She questioned the woman to lay the groundwork for her story, then she stood back and said confidently, "Now, please tell the court exactly what happened."

Suddenly the woman was telling a story Belva had never heard. "I shot him," the woman said. "I shot him because he came to arrest me." Belva tried to shush her. The woman went on. "My husband told me where the gun was. He told me to shoot anybody who tried to take me away from my home."

The courtroom became bedlam. The judge pounded his gavel. The confusion gave Belva time to think. She remembered Professor Wedgewood's words, "A lawyer's first duty is to his client." Before the judge had quieted the jurors and the spectators, Belva was saying, "Your Honor. Your Honor. Gentlemen of the jury," her voice rose above the subsiding noise. "The laws must be enforced. My client is guilty. She has committed the double offense of resisting an officer of the law, then shooting the man. But gentlemen, the District of Columbia is under the common law. That law says a woman must obey her husband. She must obey him without question. Her husband told my client to load a gun and shoot the first man who tried to force his way into the house. As a good wife, she obeyed him." Except for Belva's voice, there wasn't a sound in the courtroom.

"Gentlemen of the jury, you are trying the wrong person. I claim that under the law of the District, the husband loaded the gun and shot the officer." Belva approached the jury box. She looked into the eyes of the men sitting there. She said, "Surely, gentlemen, you would not have a woman resist her husband." The jury returned a verdict of not guilty.

The case worried Belva. That evening she couldn't concentrate on her work. Ezekiel told her, "Belva, forget about law tonight. Let's take a walk together."

Belva didn't want to go, but she knew the walk would relax her husband. Her, too, for that matter.

They walked down Ninth Street. How built up it had become since she bought the Union League Hall. Washington had grown. She looked around her. She couldn't imagine living in another city.

They waited for a carriage to pass. Ezekiel said, "That murder case bothers you, doesn't it?"

"I like to win. But I don't like to win that way. According to her story on the stand, the woman was clearly guilty. Yet I had to save her. And I had to use the only argument I could to do it."

They crossed the street. "You weren't wrong, Belva. It's the law that's wrong."

"It's a law I've tried to change with every speech I've made about equal rights."

They walked in silence. Belva said, "I think I have another fight on my hands."

"What kind of fight?" her husband asked.

"You know I've received many claim cases against the government." Ezekiel nodded. "Well, Mrs. von Cort's case comes up soon. The government has infringed on a patent for a torpedo boat her husband invented. I'm going to have to go into federal court with it."

"You haven't been admitted to the Court of Claims," Ezekiel said.

"No, but I've filed my power of attorney in the case and a certificate with the clerk of the district court.

115

Attorney Hosmer promised to move for my admittance. Everything is in order. But I'm expecting resistance from the judges in the high court." They strolled home. The walk had relaxed Belva. She fell asleep immediately.

Three days later Ezekiel accompanied Belva to the United States Court of Claims. At precisely twelve o'clock, the five justices marched in and bowed to the people. After the clerk formally opened the session, Mr. Hosmer pleaded for the admittance of Belva Ann Lockwood in the court.

When he finished, he sat down. Silence. Justice Drake broke it with slow, precise words. "Mistress Lockwood, you are a woman."

He said it with such force Belva fought a compulsion to say guilty. There was more silence. Everybody stared at her. Judge Drake said, "This cause will be continued for one week. The court will recess for ten minutes." The five judges rose together and, in perfect step, left the room.

A. A. Hosmer said to Belva, "I'm sorry, Mrs. Lockwood. I did my best."

"I know you did. Your plea for my admittance was perfect. We'll try again next week."

Mr. Hosmer said, "I'm sorry. I won't be able to. I have an important case scheduled that day."

Ezekiel asked, "Can't you ask for a continuance?"

"I'm afraid not, Mr. Lockwood."

Belva and Ezekiel were disappointed. So were Lura and DeForest. But they took courage in the fact that Belva's plea hadn't been denied outright.

The next Monday, the four of them went to the courtroom with friends. The judges walked in with the same precision they had used the week before. When the case of Lockwood was reached, Belva stood up. Justice Drake said, "Mistress Lockwood, you are a *married* woman."

Belva hadn't expected that. She stood speechless. She regained her composure. "Yes, but may it please the court, I am here with the consent of my husband." Ezekiel bowed to the judges.

"Madam, women do not speak in this courtroom. You will sit down." Justice Drake stood, "This cause will be continued until next week," he said.

The next day Belva went to Charles W. Horner. When she told him what had happened, Attorney Horner promised to present her to the court. He called on her often. Together they went over his argument. On Monday the judges looked as stern as ever. Belva thought Mr. Horner's speech would receive the same treatment as Mr. Hosmer's plea. But to her delight Mr. Horner was allowed to file his plea with the clerk before the cause of Lockwood was continued for another week.

The next week court adjourned because of the death of Judge Peck, one of the men who had sat on the bench during Belva's requests for admittance.

At dinner Belva said to Ezekiel, "I think I'm destined to spend every Monday of my life in that court while Justice Drake says, "This cause will be continued for another week."

Ezekiel laughed. "Be patient. You know how long these things take."

"I can't be patient. I have dozens of cases filed in every lower court in the district. The judges' attitude isn't fair to me, but worse, it isn't fair to my clients."

"Mr. Horner won a big victory when he received permission to file his argument. Maybe this Monday will be different."

On Monday Justice Drake didn't say anything. Instead, Justice Charles Nott told the assembly that the matter had been turned over to him for an opinion. He would give it in three weeks.

During those three weeks Belva worked compulsively. She had to stay busy to keep from going to Judge Nott to plead her case personally. She wondered how she could have wanted this business of law. It was so slow. And she was so impatient.

When the day for Judge Nott's opinion arrived, Belva went to the court alone with Lura and Mr. Horner. DeForest was working, and Ezekiel didn't feel well enough to make the trip to court. For an hour and a half Belva listened to the judge deliver his speech. He finished with: "The position which this court assumes is that under the laws and Constitution of the United States a court is without power to grant such an application and that a woman is without legal capacity to take the office of attorney. The request is *denied.*"

The judges walked out in perfect precision. They didn't look back. They didn't miss a step.

Chapter Ten

When Belva opened the door to the apartment, she saw Ezekiel by the window. He said, "I watched you walk up the street. You looked determined."

Belva threw her gloves on the table and took the pin from her hat. "I won't let those judges end my career."

"What happened?" Ezekiel asked.

Belva sat at her desk. "It took Judge Nott and his associates eight weeks to refuse my request. They wasted my time and my clients' time."

"What will you do?" Ezekiel asked.

Belva shuffled papers on her desk. "Ah, here it is." She riffled through the von Cort file. "Mrs. von Cort and I are going to invade Judge Nott's precious court," she said.

Ezekiel came to sit by her desk. "What do you mean?"

"I stopped to tell Mrs. von Cort what happened. I told her she had every right to get another attorney, but the idea upset her so much, I gave her an alternative. I'll prepare the brief, and she'll read it in court." Belva began to make notes.

"Will Judge Nott allow that?"

"He has to. A citizen has the right to represent himself."

"Even if that himself is a woman?" Ezekiel asked.

Belva smiled. "Even if that himself is a woman."

Belva devoted hours on the brief for Mrs. von Cort. By the time the day of the hearing arrived, Mrs. von Cort had read the brief aloud to Belva many times. When the two women went into the Court of Claims, they went with confidence. Mrs. von Cort conducted herself admirably. But the judges couldn't arrive at a decision. There was a continuance.

That night Belva admitted she couldn't conduct her business this way. Claims against the government arrived at her office every day. The people had the right to be represented properly.

"I'm going to have to put Judge Nott's decision to a test," she told Ezekiel while they did the dinner dishes.

"What will you do?"

"The *Webster Raines* claim case is ready to file. I'm

going to tell him and his wife what I'm up against and ask them if they will let me try to represent them."

"You really like these claim cases, don't you?" Ezekiel said.

"I'd like to specialize in them."

"I'll give up dentistry and help you," Ezekiel said. "I'm too old to be on my feet all day pulling teeth. I can get a job as a claims agent and be outside more. What do you think?"

"I think it's a marvelous idea. You can investigate the claims, and I'll bring them to court. If I ever get into court, that is."

Ezekiel said, "I'll apply for a job tomorrow."

"And I'll go see Mrs. Raines."

Mr. Raines wouldn't agree to Belva's plan. He said if her challenge didn't work, he would have to change attorneys. It could take weeks, maybe months before the new lawyer was ready. He wanted the matter settled now. But Mrs. Raines insisted Belva take the case. The Raines argued. Mrs. Raines was adamant. Belva stayed.

The night before she was due to appear before Judge Nott, Belva was nervous. The thought of facing the judge again frightened her and, to add to her uneasiness, Ezekiel was bedridden again.

Belva went for the doctor. After he examined Ezekiel, the doctor came into the kitchen where Belva waited with Lura. "Mrs. Lockwood, your husband is a very sick man," he said.

Lura asked, "How sick, Doctor?"

"He has an incurable disease." The women gasped. "I'm sorry to have to tell you this, ladies, but I've learned that in cases like these it's better to prepare the family."

"How long does he have?" Lura asked.

"He may live only a few months, or he may go on for years."

"Have you told my husband?"

"There's no need for him to know. Unless you feel differently, of course."

Belva fought tears. "We won't tell him. We'll go on as before." She walked with the doctor to the door. "Thank you for coming," she said.

"Send for me any time, Mrs. Lockwood. I've left pills with your husband. He's to take them if he has pain."

"Will he suffer much?" Belva asked.

"That depends on how long . . . that depends on how long he lives," the man said before he started down the stairs.

Lura asked, "Do you want me to stay?" Her body was filling out. She would have to stop working soon to have her baby.

Belva said, "No, you go home and rest. I'll be fine."

After Lura left, Belva went to the bedroom. Ezekiel was asleep. She was relieved. She didn't feel ready to face him.

Belva lay awake filled with doubts about her ability to keep the secret from Ezekiel. But she had to do it. The doctor was right. There was no need for her husband to know how sick he was. The knowledge might shorten his life.

Alone in the dark, Belva worried about the expenses of their home. And the doctor's bills — they would take most of what she earned. She and Ezekiel had a little money saved. That would carry them over until more of her cases started to pay. She had dozens on file. She thought about Judge Nott and his associates. She had to make them listen. But how, when they wouldn't let her open her mouth?

Belva thought about the Court of Claims. Getting in there wasn't the answer to her problem. Some day she would have to appeal one of her cases to the Supreme Court of the United States. What then? As long as she could do only half a job, she couldn't expect people to come to her for help. She turned over and tried to sleep. It was no use. She got up and warmed a cup of milk. A thought occurred to her. She ran to her office. She lit the lamp and pulled a book from the shelf. She remembered reading something years ago. What was it? She took another book and riffled through the pages. Nothing. It was almost dawn before she found what she wanted. A few words. She read them slowly, "Any attorney in good standing before the highest court of any State or Territory for the space of three years shall be admitted to this court when presented by a member of this bar."

Belva read the words repeatedly. It didn't say any man or any male citizen. It said any attorney in good standing. She was a member of the bar of the Supreme Court of the District of Columbia. She could become a member of the Supreme Court of the United States, if she remained in good standing. But this was only the end of 1874. It would be almost two years before she filled the three-year requirement. "I've waited all my life," she thought. "I can wait two more years." The sun came up. Belva went to see if Ezekiel was awake.

"You're up early," he said when she entered the bedroom. "Nervous about Judge Nott?"

Belva fluffed up his pillows. "A little. How do you feel?"

"Better. What did the doctor say?"

Belva went to open the drapes. Little light came in. She was glad her husband couldn't see her hands tremble. "He said you'll be fine. Want some breakfast?"

"Just coffee and toast. What time are you due in court?"

"Nine o'clock. And I have a feeling we'll be out by nine-o-five."

"Belva, why do you drive yourself? There's no need."

"There is a need. Legally there's no reason why I can't practice in the Court of Claims, just as there's no reason why I can't elect my public officials. In both cases, my rights are denied me."

After she gave Ezekiel his breakfast, Belva dressed to meet Mr. and Mrs. Raines. She was exhausted. Her eyes burned from the lack of sleep. Her throat ached from holding back tears. She knew the tears would come. She hoped they wouldn't come in Judge Nott's courtroom.

The Raines met her in the courthouse. After the judges marched in, the clerk declared the court in session. "Webster M. Raines et ux versus the United States of America," he said.

Belva stood up. "Your Honor, my clients . . ."

Judge Nott banged his gavel. "Madam, what are you doing in my courtroom?"

"Your Honor, I represent Mr. Raines and his wife."

"Mrs. Lockwood, if you dare speak, I shall hold you in contempt."

Belva opened her mouth. The words she had read during the night came to her. "An attorney in good standing for three years." A contempt charge would ruin her chances. Belva sat down.

Mr. Raines jumped to his feet. "Your Honor, Mrs. Lockwood is a capable attorney. I hired her to represent me, and I insist she be allowed to do it."

Judge Nott said, "Mr. Raines, sit down."

"Where are my rights?"

"Your rights lie in a lawyer who is qualified to represent you in this court."

"I demand that Mrs. Lockwood represent me."

The gavel pounded again. "Mr. Raines, I shall hold you in contempt."

Webster Raines moved toward the bench. Belva held him back. She nodded toward the door. She left with her clients.

When they reached the corridor, Mr. Raines said, "It isn't right. If you practice in the lower courts, you should be able to practice here."

Belva leaned against the wall, weak from fatigue. "If Judge Nott had his way, I wouldn't practice in the lower courts either."

"What do we do now?" Mrs. Raines asked.

Belva said, "We'll have to get another attorney."

Mr. Raines said, "I told a lawyer a couple of weeks ago about our case. He said he could win it for us. We'll get him."

Belva was skeptical of such a claim. No lawyer

could be certain of the outcome of this case. She questioned the man's qualifications, but the Raineses wanted to hire him. When she couldn't dissuade them Belva agreed to work with him. "I'll meet with him tomorrow and discuss the case. I'm sorry about this morning," she said.

Mrs. Raines asked, "Can we see you home? You look so tired."

"Thank you, I'll be all right."

Belva boarded a horsecar. She wondered if she could stay awake until she got home. She climbed the stairs to the apartment. Ezekiel was asleep. Belva slumped to the couch. Tears came, then uncontrollable sobs. She buried her face in the cushions so she wouldn't wake Ezekiel. He wouldn't learn the truth of his illness from her.

After the first of the year Ezekiel felt well enough to go back to work. The activity gave the Lockwoods hope. And the money Ezekiel earned helped ease their financial woes. Belva resented the people who kept her from practicing in the higher courts. Their prejudice forced her to seek out a living writing wills, filing deeds or serving notices. But Belva knew no way to rectify the injustice. She could only wait for her three years as an attorney in good standing to pass.

She told no one except Ezekiel about the rule that would allow her to practice before the Supreme Court of the United States. Someone might change the "any attorney" to any male attorney before she fulfilled her three-year requirement.

Within weeks Ezekiel stopped working again. He was often discouraged. He spent more and more time in bed. "What's the matter with me? What are we going to do for money?" he asked Belva.

"We'll manage," Belva told him. "And you'll be all right." But he wasn't. By the time Lura had her baby, Ezekiel was bedridden, and he had guessed that he would never get well. He held the new baby: "I shall never see her grow up," he said. He turned to Belva, "We must enjoy whatever days we have left together," he told her. Belva agreed.

The night before she was due to appear in the Court of Claims with Mr. and Mrs. Raines and their attorney, Belva sat beside Ezekiel's bed making notes.

Ezekiel asked, "How do you feel about appearing before Judge Nott after all these months?"

"Appearing before him is about all I'll do. I can't say a word," Belva put down her pencil. "I wish I felt more confident about this other man."

"Isn't he competent?"

"He's competent. But he takes an hour to say what I can say in minutes. He could use Professor Wedgewood's advice. 'Say what you mean then sit down.'"

"I should think that after your trouble with Professor Wedgewood, you wouldn't want to quote anything he said."

"I'll always listen to good advice, Ezekiel. I don't care who gives it." Belva got up. "I'll get your medicine."

Ezekiel stopped her. "We'll have to hire someone. You can't handle your law practice and the house and me."

Belva had thought of hiring help, but they couldn't afford it. Still she needed someone. Her schedule exhausted her. "We'll get a helper when they let me practice in the Supreme Court of the United States. My position will demand it." Ezekiel smiled. "Just one more year," Belva said happily. Her husband's smile faded. "I'll make it," she said. She put her hand on his. "And so will you."

Belva held back tears. "I'll get your medicine," she said.

She met Mr. and Mrs. Raines and their attorney in the courtroom the next morning. When Judge Nott entered, he looked over his glasses at Belva. She pretended not to see him. The man beside her rose to present his case. Her case really. That evening Belva went home exhausted from the strain of her court-enforced silence.

By the middle of the second day, she doubted they could win the case. The next day she learned she was right. Judge Nott ruled that Mr. and Mrs. Raines didn't have a legitimate claim against the government. Mr. Raines angrily discharged his attorney.

Belva had mixed feelings about the outcome. She had wanted the Raineses to win. Still, as they asked her what they should do, she was glad they hadn't won. This was the case she would take to the Supreme Court. By the time its turn came up on the calendar, she would have her three years as a practicing attorney. "We'll appeal to the Supreme Court," Belva said in answer to their questions.

Mr. Raines said, "That will mean still another attorney."

"It doesn't have to," Belva said. Mr. and Mrs. Raines stared at her. Belva told them about her plan and swore them to secrecy.

"Do you think it will work?" Mrs. Raines asked.

"It has to work. The rule has only thirty-four words. They can't be misinterpreted," Belva said.

"It seems as though this case has gone on forever," Mr. Raines said.

"Many cases do. There's a delay, a continuance or an unexpected ruling. But the Supreme Court is the top. We'll win or lose there."

Mrs. Raines said, "Very well, Mrs. Lockwood. You file for us."

"Thank you, Mrs. Raines."

Mr. Raines said, "I hope there's no surprise ruling."

Belva shuddered at the thought.

Chapter Eleven

Belva and Ezekiel greeted 1876 surrounded by Lura, DeForest and their children. It was a quiet celebration, but a happy one for Belva. It had been more than a year since the doctor told her about Ezekiel's illness and, although he was bedridden, he suffered little pain. The doctor was amazed at Ezekiel's ability to fight the illness. There was no reason to be pessimistic when Belva attended the National Woman Suffrage Association Convention several weeks later.

After the first day of meetings, Belva told Ezekiel, "Susan can't get to Washington for the convention this year."

"Is she ill?"

"No, she's making speeches in the Midwest. But she'll be at the country's centennial in July."

"Will you tell her then about the rule that will get you admitted to the Supreme Court?"

"I'm not going to Philadelphia," Belva said.

"Why not?" Ezekiel asked. He answered his own question. "You don't want to leave me." Ezekiel held her hand. "I want you to go."

"I can't," Belva said.

"Of course you can. We'll hire a housekeeper. She can take care of things while you're away."

Belva needed help whether she went to Philadelphia or not. Her schedule exhausted her. And she worried about leaving Ezekiel alone while she was in court. "I'll look for someone tomorrow, but I'm not going to Philadelphia," she said.

"We'll see," Ezekiel said.

Within a week Belva found Martha. She came to the Lockwoods' on Monday and by Saturday Belva wondered how she had managed without her. Martha took over the household chores. And Lura came to work a few hours a day in the office. Belva realized how tired she was. "I must have lived on reserve power for months," she told Ezekiel.

"Now you can rest for your trip to Philadelphia," he said.

"I'm not going."

"You'll go," Ezekiel said. Belva protested. "You'll go," he repeated.

135

Through the spring members of the National Woman Suffrage Association made plans to interrupt the celebration in Philadelphia. The women in New York sent word to Washington that they would make people aware of the discrimination against women, and they would do it any way they could. It sounded ominous and exciting to Belva, and when Ezekiel continued to insist she make the trip, Belva decided to go. On July 1 she gave last-minute instructions to Martha and Lura and took the train to Philadelphia.

When she saw Susan, Belva asked what the group had decided to do. Susan said, "We're going to present the Declaration of Women's Rights that Elizabeth Stanton and Matilda Gage prepared."

"When?" Belva asked.

"I think right after the reading of Thomas Jefferson's Declaration of Independence would be the most meaningful moment. But we'll watch for the best opportunity. When it comes, we'll move quickly."

The Fourth of July dawned hot and humid. Despite the heat, Independence Hall was almost full by the time Belva arrived. She found a seat, waved to Susan and waited for the ceremonies to begin.

At ten o'clock the band played "Hail Columbia." When the music stopped, Thomas Ferry welcomed the people, then a man read Thomas Jefferson's Declara-

tion of Independence. Belva looked to see what Susan was doing. She and the women around her sat motionless. The speaker finished. The band leader said, "Ladies and Gentlemen, the Brazilian national anthem, in honor of the Brazilian emperor."

There was activity at Susan's place. Several women pushed through the crowd until they stood in front of Thomas Ferry. Susan placed her document in his hand and left. On the way to the door, the women threw pamphlets to the crowd. People scrambled over each other to get a copy.

Belva grabbed one in mid-air. It was a replica of the declaration that Susan had given to Mr. Ferry. Belva read it. It ended, "We ask of our rulers at this hour no special favors, no special privileges, no special legislation. We ask justice, we ask equality, we ask that all the civil and political rights that belong to citizens of the United States be guaranteed to us and our daughters forever." Belva ran after Susan.

By the time she got outside, Susan was on the bandstand reading the Declaration of Women's Rights she had presented. When she finished, the women went to the Unitarian church for a suffragist rally. Belva made a speech. She told about the injustice and the inequality she had experienced as a lawyer. "Don't just talk about discrimination," she said. "Fight it. If you don't, our daughters will experience this same

138

agonizing, shameful treatment on our country's two hundredth birthday."

The rally lasted past five o'clock. Exhausted, Belva returned to her room to bathe and change before she joined the others for discussions. She learned that some of the women would stay in the city to dispense information to the thousands of visitors who were expected to visit Philadelphia during the summer. Belva wished she could stay, but she had to get back to Ezekiel, and she had to prepare for her presentation to the justices of the Supreme Court. She decided to leave the work in Philadelphia to others and continue her fight in Washington.

When Belva saw Ezekiel, she was startled by his appearance. She had been gone only a few days, but he looked so much thinner, so much weaker than when she left. Or was it that she hadn't wanted to admit earlier how much his body had deteriorated. He was always so cheerful, always so helpful, she hadn't noticed the day-to-day changes. When she asked him how he felt, Ezekiel confessed that he had increased his dosage of pain pills. He had done it before she left, and Martha had helped him keep it from her. "Ezekiel, you should have told me. I would have stayed with you."

"That's why I didn't tell you." Belva scolded him, but he only smiled.

"You're an unusual man, Ezekiel Lockwood," she said.

The day after she returned to Washington, Belva went to see the Honorable Albert Riddle, a staunch supporter of equal rights for women. He agreed to present her to the Supreme Court, and Belva visited him often. She insisted they go over details again and again until Mr. Riddle lost his patience.

"Mrs. Lockwood, there's nothing to worry about. You said yourself the rule can't be misinterpreted."

Belva said, "I'm sorry. I'm just impatient."

"The time will come. Keep busy. It will help."

Belva followed his advice. She filed more cases. She continued her work for suffrage. She lobbied for the congressional bills she supported. She even started to think about selling the Union League Hall. The idea had crossed her mind occasionally, but she hadn't thought about it seriously. However, after the summer heat turned the apartment into a hot box, she decided a house with a yard would be better for Ezekiel. She could roll his bed outside on nice days. The change might help him, and an office on the street floor would be more convenient for her clients. During her daily business around Washington, Belva began keeping an eye open for another place to live.

When the Supreme Court resumed its sessions in October 1876, Belva and A. G. Riddle were there to see the nine black-robed justices walk from their chambers to the rostrum in front of the room. Morrison I. Waite, the chief justice, sat in the center under a purple canopy and a gold eagle that held the words "In God We Trust" in its beak.

The clerk announced, "All ye who have business with the Honorable, the Supreme Court of the United States are admonished to draw near and pay attention, for the Court is now sitting." Belva clasped her hands to keep them still.

Mr. Riddle rose, "Your Honors, I represent Mrs. Belva Lockwood, attorney-at-law. We move for her admittance to your Court." The nine men stared at Belva. "I have the necessary papers. I am certain you will find everything in order," Mr. Riddle said. The judges continued to stare. Belva's hand went to her throat. It played nervously with the lace at her neck. Mr. Riddle handed the papers to the clerk, who gave them to the chief justice. The judges conferred. Belva wondered if they could hear her heart pound.

The chief justice said, "We will take this under advisement until next Monday at twelve o'clock," he said.

"What is there to take under advisement?" Belva asked Mr. Riddle. "The brief is simply worded. The affidavits of my good standing at the bar are in order."

Mr. Riddle said he didn't know and told her again to

be patient. Belva went home confused and angry. She told Ezekiel, "It looks as though I'm back on the 'continued until next Monday' circuit."

"What happened?" her husband asked.

Belva told him what Justice Waite had said. "I hope they don't take eight weeks to make up their minds the way the judges did at the Court of Claims."

At precisely noon the next Monday, the nine judges walked to their places. Without preliminaries, Chief Justice Waite said, "By the uniform practice of the court, from its organization to the present time, and by the fair construction of its rule, *none but men* are admitted to practice before it as attorneys and counsellors. This is in accordance with immemorial usage in England, and the law and practice in all the states until within a recent period; and the court does not feel called upon to make a change, until such a change is required by statute, or a more extended practice in the highest courts of the States.

"As this court knows no English precedent for the admission of women to the bar, it *declines* to admit, unless there shall be a more extended public opinion or special legislation."

Belva's shoulders slumped. Mr. Riddle touched her arm. They walked out. Outside, Belva asked angrily, "What does he mean there's no English precedent? What about Queen Elizabeth? Or Anne, the Countess

142

of Pembroke? She was sheriff of Westmoreland, for heaven's sake. Those judges are wrong. Women have practiced in high courts before."

"Perhaps, but the judges have spoken. You must ask Congress to pass a law to admit you to the Supreme Court or practice only in the lower courts."

"I'm as capable in my profession as any man," Belva said.

"But unless you can convince Congress to pass a law, you won't have the opportunity to prove it."

They walked down the stairs. Belva became more angry. Special legislation would cost money and time. She had little of either. She remembered what she had said in Philadelphia. "Don't just talk about discrimination. Fight it. If you don't, our daughters will still experience this same agonizing, shameful treatment on our country's two hundredth birthday." The judges' decision was outright discrimination. She had to fight it.

When they reached the sidewalk, Belva said, "I'll let you know what my plans will be."

Attorney Riddle boarded the horsecar that stopped beside him. Belva walked home, reluctant to tell Ezekiel the news.

Chapter Twelve

Belva *hired an* attorney to represent Mr. and Mrs. Raines in the Supreme Court and tried to raise money for her new battle with the judges.

"I'll sell the Union League Hall," she told Ezekiel when she had no success.

"Where will we live?" Ezekiel asked.

"Prices have soared since I bought the hall. I should make enough profit to buy a house and pay my expenses," Belva told him. His pain-filled eyes never failed to move her. "Don't worry, Ezekiel. I'll win this time."

"You always say that."

"I know," Belva said.

She went to her office and got to work on a bill to present to Congress. It stated . . . "any *woman* who shall have been a member of the bar of the highest court of any State or Territory or of the supreme court of the District of Columbia for the space of three years, and shall have maintained a good standing before such court, and who shall be a person of good moral character shall, on motion and the production of such record, be admitted to practice before the Supreme Court of the United States."

Belva took the bill to Benjamin F. Butler the next day. "Mr. Butler, you've worked for women's rights for many years. Now I hope you'll help me in my fight for justice." She put the draft of her bill on his desk. "Will you introduce this in the House of Representatives?"

Mr. Butler glanced at the papers. "I'd like to help, Mrs. Lockwood, but I already have so many bills to introduce. And this is a presidential year. I don't see where I can find time to get support."

"You introduce it. I'll get support," Belva said.

Benjamin Butler read the bill, "Very well, I'll do it. But I don't hold much hope for its passage."

"You will by the time I finish," Belva said.

Belva used every spare moment to visit Congressmen for whom she had lobbied. She asked for help. Many were sympathetic, but they were too involved in the presidential election to give her much time.

"See me after the election," they told her. But voting day didn't free them from their commitments. The electoral votes of Louisiana, Florida, South Carolina and Oregon were disputed, and both parties charged their opponents with fraud. For weeks no one knew whether Rutherford B. Hayes or Samuel J. Tilden would be the next President of the United States.

While the debate progressed, Belva sold the Union League Hall and moved to 619 F Street N.W. It was a spacious house, a pleasant house, much more suited to her present needs than the Union League Hall.

When Congress assembled in December 1876, Mr. Butler introduced Belva's bill to the House. But it didn't receive enough votes to get out of committee. Belva resolved on the spot to get more support and have the bill introduced again when Congress reconvened.

At the National Woman Suffrage Association Convention in January, Belva reported on her unsuccessful bid for the Supreme Court. "To arrive at the same conclusion with these judges," she told her audience, "it is not necessary to understand constitutional law, nor the history of English jurisprudence, nor the inductive or deductive modes of reasoning, as no such profound learning or processes of thought were involved in that decision, which was simply this: There is no precedent for admitting a woman to practice in the Supreme Court of the United States, hence Mrs. Lockwood's application cannot be considered."

Ezekiel read the speech in the *Ballot-Box*. He said, "Not many people have courage to say what you did about those judges."

"I only told the truth. Those men didn't have to think to reach their decision. They didn't want a woman to practice in their Court, so they said there was no precedent. Blackstone gives several precedents of women in the English courts."

"You said that in your speech."

"Do they have all that in there?" Belva reached for the paper.

Ezekiel held it from her. "They have that and more." He read, "As Mrs. Lockwood — tall, well-proportioned, with dark hair and eyes, regular features, in velvet dress and train, with becoming indignation at such injustice — marched up and down the platform and rounded out her glowing periods, she might have fairly represented the Italian Portia at the bar of Venice. No more effective speech was ever made from the platform." Ezekiel looked up from the paper. "You don't have dark eyes," he said.

Belva took the paper from him and read the article. Had she marched? She put down the paper. She had been angry enough to march.

After an electoral commission gave its decision on the election, Rutherford B. Hayes was inaugurated President of the United States on March 5, 1877. By that time Ezekiel lived with constant pain. Belva spent as much time with him as she could. She was at his side when he died April 23, 1877.

After the funeral a woman told Belva, "It's unfortunate you have to stop work on your bill."

"I can't stop. John Glover has already promised to re-introduce it in December."

The woman looked horrified. "Surely you'll observe a mourning period."

"If I had died, my husband would have continued to work."

"It's different for a man," the woman said. "He has to earn a living."

"I'll mourn in my own way," Belva said angrily.

To Belva grief was a private thing. She continued her court appearances, her lobbying and her speeches. Ezekiel would have wanted it that way.

Through the summer and fall Belva went to see scores of representatives. Some listened to her arguments in favor of her bill. Others weren't so kind. "The next thing you know, you women will want to rule the country," they said. It was the standard remark from men who were afraid to give women their rights.

The day John M. Glover of Missouri introduced Bill

No. 1077 titled "A bill to relieve certain disabilities of women," Belva sat in the gallery of the House of Representatives. She heard the bill put on the agenda for discussion. By the time the session ended the bill had been sent to the Committee on the Judiciary for debate. This time Belva was determined to get enough votes to get it out of committee.

She talked to groups of Representatives and visited them individually. More of them said they would support her efforts. When the House adjourned for the Christmas holiday, she felt Bill 1077 had a chance.

Belva spent Christmas with Lura, DeForest and the children. She appreciated their efforts to help her through the holidays without Ezekiel. But she was glad when the holiday season finished and she could go back to work. It kept her mind on the future instead of the past.

When the House reconvened, the Committee on the Judiciary asked Belva to appear before it. One congressman asked her why the bill was necessary. "To give me rights that are already mine," she said. She told him about the rule she found that should allow her to practice before the Supreme Court. "If I were a man, my plea for admission would have been granted." The man asked more questions. Belva answered them. When she finished, the committee returned the bill to the House.

On February 21, 1878, Benjamin Butler and John Glover argued for passage of the bill. They asked for the yeas and nays. Mr. White from Pennsylvania asked that the bill be read again before the chief clerk took a poll. Belva listened to more questions and heard someone ask for one more reading. Everything took so long. Belva wondered how anything ever got done. Finally the bill went up for votes.

Belva tried to keep track of them. Her eyes went from one man, then to another as each cast his vote. She moved to the edge of her chair and clutched the rail in front of her. The yeas appeared to outnumber the nays. Did they? The clerk said, "One hundred sixty-nine yeas, eighty-seven nays, and thirty-six abstaining." Belva jumped to her feet. Bill 1077 had cleared the House. It was sent to the Senate's Committee on the Judiciary.

Belva went to Lura's house to celebrate and to meet the press. "The Senate is next, Mrs. Lockwood. How many senators do you have on your side?" a reporter asked.

"That's hard to know. Let's say I have to do a lot of convincing."

A man from the *Star* asked, "What are your immediate plans, Mrs. Lockwood?"

"My immediate plans are the passage of my bill and my admittance to the Supreme Court. But, of course, I have cases to take care of. In fact, I just filed one in the federal court of Baltimore, Maryland — *Royuello v. Attoche.* The matter comes before the court in October."

A reporter said, "You don't have the right to appear in the federal court of Baltimore, do you, Mrs. Lockwood?"

Belva said, "Sir, I have the right. I just haven't been given permission."

The men laughed. "Then you have another fight on your hands."

"That depends on the judge," Belva said.

After the newspapermen left, DeForest asked Belva, "How many senators *do* you have on your side?"

"I'm not certain. Of course, I can rely on Aaron Sargent and George Hoar and Joseph McDonald and Mr. Riddle. I don't know about the others. But most of them will get a visit from me soon."

During the next month Belva stopped senators in the halls and on the street corners. She went to their offices. She called on them in their homes. Still, despite her lobbying, on March 18 Belva heard George Edmunds of Vermont, chairman of the Committee on the Judiciary, give an adverse report in the Senate.

"The committee thinks that this bill would make a distinction in favor of women, instead of removing a disability," he said. "There is no disability now whatever. It all depends upon the discretion of the court, and the bill commands the court to admit women under circumstances where the courts would not be bound to admit men. We are of the opinion, therefore, that no legislation is required. I suggest that the bill be indefinitely postponed."

Aaron Sargent jumped to his feet, "I ask that the bill go on the calendar," he said.

Belva held her breath. The vice president said, "The bill will be placed on the calendar with the committee's adverse report." Belva sighed. Bill No. 1077 was still alive.

After the Senate recessed, Belva hurried to Aaron Sargent's office. "We'll have to change the wording," he said when she entered. "The committee feels your bill asks special favors for women."

"I know," Belva said. "The change of words won't be difficult. I'm more concerned with their idea that no legislation is necessary because the admittance of women is up to the courts."

Senator Sargent nodded. "We'll have to show that the Court refused to admit you without a valid reason."

Belva asked, "Do you think it would help if my colleagues signed a petition? There are dozens of attorneys who have told me they felt the Supreme Court's decision was unfair."

"It might help," Aaron Sargent said.

"I'll get started right away," Belva said. When she finished Belva had the signatures of a hundred and fifty-five lawyers on a petition asking that she be allowed to practice before the Supreme Court.

On April 22 Mr. Sargent entered an amendment to Bill 1077. The chief clerk read it, "The amendment is to insert: That no person shall be excluded from practicing as an attorney and counselor at law from any court of the United States on account of sex."

When he finished, Aaron Sargent spoke of Belva's acceptance by members of the legal profession. He said that many states were admitting women to the bar, and his own state of California had passed such a law within the past two weeks. He turned to the gallery when he said: "There is no reason in principle why women should not be admitted to this profession or the profession of medicine, provided they have the learning to enable them to be useful in those professions, and useful to themselves. Where is the propriety in opening our colleges, our high institutions of learning, or any institutions of learning to women, and then when they have acquired in the race with men the cultivation of higher employments to shut them out? There certainly is none." Belva wanted to applaud. She held back. She didn't want to be asked to leave.

Mr. Sargent went on to point out the unfairness of a profession that would allow a woman to practice before a lower court then make her turn her clients over to a male attorney when the case had to be carried to a higher court.

Mr. Garland asked, "Can't a court of the United States admit women on their own motion?"

Mr. Sargent said, "To my knowledge, it can. But the chief justice has asked for special legislation, and Mrs. Lockwood is seeking it."

After more arguments the bill was sent back to the Committee on the Judiciary with the amendment. When it returned on May 20, Belva heard Mr. Thurman of Ohio read: "There is no law prohibiting a court from admitting a woman to practice law; and . . . therefore, there is no necessity for this bill; and for that, as well as other reasons which I need not enumerate, the committee recommends the indefinite postponement of the bill."

Mr. Sargent said, "I would like to ask the senator from Ohio if the committee is not aware that the chief justice, in deciding against the admission of a lady applicant, said that the Supreme Court would wait for legislation." The point had been brought up before. Belva wondered if senators ever listened to what their colleagues said.

Mr. Thurman told Mr. Sargent, "I really am not

154

aware of any remark made by the chief justice. All we can do is report what we find the law to be in our judgment, and that we have done."

Mr. Hoar from Massachusetts came to Mr. Sargent's aid, but the bill was put aside for a week. When it came up on May 29 Belva knew it had to pass then or wait another year. Mr. Sargent asked for a vote. Several men said there wasn't time to read the bill and take votes. Mr. Sargent called again for the yeas and nays. His request was denied. The bill was put on the calendar until the next session of Congress.

Belva left the gallery angry and disappointed and yet relieved. Bill 1077 hadn't passed, but it was still on the calendar. She had feared the words "indefinitely postponed."

When Belva told Lura what happened, she said, "The bill has received a lot of publicity from the press, Mother. People are aware of your fight. Maybe you can get them interested enough to write to their senators about it."

Belva put her feet up on the ottoman and rubbed the back of her neck. "I'll think about it," she said.

Lura asked, "Why don't you have dinner with us tonight? It will give you a chance to see the children. They keep asking where their grandmother is. It's hard to explain that she's disappeared into the caverns of the Senate building." Belva smiled and shook her head. "Mother, you look so discouraged. The visit will help you," Lura said.

Belva finally agreed to go, but she came home as soon as her grandchildren went to bed. She had briefs to work on.

Through the summer Belva tried to make senators understand the need for the legislation. The newsmen helped her. They wrote more and more stories about her struggle. When she met one of the newsmen, she thanked him.

He said, "The other men and I talked it over. We like the way you battle odds. We're going to cover your activities as often as our editors let us."

Belva remembered what the chief justice had said when he refused to admit her, ". . . unless there shall be a more extended public opinion or special legislation." Belva had focused on special legislation, but if that failed she would turn to public opinion to win her rights, and the newspaper stories would help her.

When Belva went to Maryland in October, the courtroom was crowded. But the people didn't hear her plead her case in federal court. Instead they heard Judge Magruder say: "God has set a bound for woman. Man was created first and woman after a part of him. Like the sun and the moon in their different orbits, the great seas have their bounds; and the eternal hills and rocks that are set over them cannot be removed. In the statutes of the State there are only masculine pronouns. A woman belongs in the home to wait on her husband and children."

Belva grasped the table in front of her. When the judge finished, she stood up. "Your Honor, you have misunderstood the principal point of my brief . . ."

"Be seated, Mrs. Lockwood."

"But Your Honor . . . ?"

"Madam, you will sit down," Judge Magruder said.

"May I have permission to speak?"

"A woman will not speak while I am holding a hearing."

"Then may I speak to the crowd at the noon recess?" Belva asked, determined to plead her case to the people.

Judge Magruder shrugged. "Please yourself, madam."

Belva left the courtroom. When she returned at noon, the doors were locked. People surrounded her. Belva grasped the opportunity to win public opinion. She walked to a portico at the side of the courthouse and told the crowd of Judge Magruder's shameful behavior.

The story about Belva's speech and Judge Magruder's action went out to dozens of newspapers. And

when she read about it in the *New York Times*, Belva felt that if she lost her fight in Congress, she would win it through the people.

After Belva returned to Washington, Aaron Sargent was taken ill and his doctor ordered complete rest. Belva went to Joseph McDonald of Indiana and asked him to urge passage of her bill. He refused. "It's Senator Sargent's bill, Mrs. Lockwood. We'll have to wait until he returns," he said.

"If the bill comes up and there's no one to urge its passage, it may be shelved indefinitely. I've worked so hard, Mr. McDonald. I can't let it go now."

The senator puffed his cigar. Belva waited. Finally he said, "Very well, I'll speak for your bill, but I won't do it alone."

"I'll get someone to help you. I'll get Senator Hoar," Belva said quickly.

Senator McDonald said, "He's a good man. You get Hoar and I'll go along." Belva thanked him and hurried to George Hoar's office.

He was willing to argue in favor of the bill, if Belva received permission from Senator Sargent. The arrangements were made. Belva's confidence grew. She had two powerful senators on her side. And when Senator Sargent returned to the Senate before her bill appeared on the calendar, Belva felt certain of victory.

But when Bill 1077 came up on February 7, 1879,

her doubts returned. There were more arguments. She resented the laws that made her sit mute while others pleaded her case. The talk on the floor continued. The senators recessed for lunch. Belva waited in the gallery. She couldn't eat. Occasionally a man came back to his desk then left again. A janitor came to empty the spittoons. He checked the inkwells. Mundane jobs performed in a room where her future might be decided within minutes.

At one-thirty the men began to stroll back. Senators Sargent, Hoar and McDonald hurried in and talked beside Senator Sargent's desk. After the clerk called the men to order, George Hoar asked permission to speak. He told his colleagues the bill wasn't "merely a bill to admit women to the privilege of engaging in a particular profession; it is a bill to secure to the citizens of the United States the right to select his counsel and that is all." When he finished Mr. Edmunds surprised Belva by calling for the yeas and nays.

The result was thirty-nine yeas, twenty nays and seventeen abstaining. The bill had passed. The three men who had worked for it smiled at Belva. She wanted to run and hug them, but she was afraid if she tried to stand her legs would not support her.

Chapter Thirteen

For days after Bill 1077 passed, newspapers arrived in Belva's office with the story. The Washington *Star* said, "The credit for this victory belongs to Mrs. Belva Lockwood, of this city, having been refused admission to the bar of the United States Supreme Court, appealed to Congress, and by dint of hard work has finally succeeded in having her bill passed by both houses."

The New York *Nation* printed, "The bill was carried through merely by the energetic advocacy of Senators McDonald, Sargent and Hoar, whose oratorical efforts were reenforced by the presence of Mrs. Lockwood. After the struggle was over, all the senators who advocated the bill were made recipients of bouquets,

161

while the three senators whose names we have given received large baskets of flowers. This is a pleasing omen of that purification of legal business which it is hoped will flow from the introduction of women to the courts. It was not flowers that used to be distributed at Washington and Albany in the old corrupt times, among legislators, in testimony of gratitude of their votes. Let us hope that venal legislation at Washington will be extirpated by the rise of this beautiful custom."

And the *Havre Republican* from Havre de Grace, Maryland, recalled Belva's appearance in Judge Magruder's court. It wrote, "How humiliated poor old Judge Magruder must feel, since the congress of the United States paid the woman whom he forbade to open her mouth in his august presence, in his little court, so much consideration to pass an act opening to her the doors of the Supreme Court of the United States. All honor to the brave woman, who by her own unaided efforts thus achieved honor, fortune and fame — the just rewards of her own true worth."

There were stories in the *New York Times*, the New York *World*, the Washington *Post*, the Philadelphia *Public Ledger*. Each day brought more newspapers with more stories. There wasn't a state that didn't know about the victory.

On March 3, 1879, Belva went with Albert G. Riddle to the Supreme Court where two and a half years before she had been refused admittance. Now Justice Morrison I. Waite administered the oath of office. "I do solemnly swear," Belva repeated after him, "that I will demean myself as an attorney and counselor of this court uprightly and according to law, and that I will support the Constitution of the United States." Three days later, on a motion by Thomas J. Durant, she was admitted to the Court of Claims. Her triumph was complete.

In the spring the Universal Peace Union met in Washington. Delegates from all over the United States and Europe attended the meetings presided over by Alfred Love of Philadelphia. Belva met Mr. Love and liked him. She threw her energy into the Peace Union meetings and became its secretary. She spoke of the need for peace with the same zeal she gave to women's equal rights. A dynamic speaker, she was in demand at banquets, conventions, bazaars, any place where she could reach people with her message of peace and equal rights.

Belva gave her speeches between court appearances. She accepted any kind of case, but the claim cases were her favorites. She became a familiar figure in the Court of Claims, where she presented briefs and depositions and submitted questions almost daily to Judge Nott and his four associates.

Lura asked her mother to give up some of her

activities. Belva wouldn't hear of it. "Mother, you're almost fifty years old. You have to slow down."

"Why?" Belva asked while she stuffed folders into her briefcase.

"Because older people need rest."

"Nonsense," Belva said, and hurried out the door.

At the National Woman Suffrage Association Convention in January, the members chose Belva to represent the women of Washington at the Republican Convention in Chicago in June. After she told Lura about the appointment, Belva said, "I suppose you're going to try to talk me out of it."

"No, DeForest has convinced me you'll be happy only when you're working," Lura said. She took a letter from her desk. "Here's another demand on your time. A man in Alabama wants you to present his request for admittance to the Supreme Court."

"Why me?" Belva asked. She read the letter from a man named Samuel R. Lowry. He explained that he had lost one of his cases in the Supreme Court of Alabama, and he wanted to take it to the Supreme Court of the United States. He went on to say he felt that Belva would understand his situation. They both had experienced prejudice and discrimination all their lives. She was a woman. He was black.

Belva wrote to Mr. Lowry, "I shall be honored to move for your admittance."

On February 2, 1880, Samuel Lowry stood beside Belva while she spoke for him in Court. "Your Honors, I am a member of this bar, and Mr. Lowry is an attorney in good standing before the highest court of Alabama," Belva told the nine justices. "I move for his admittance." The judges examined the affidavits she had prepared. They conferred. Belva felt certain of a continuance, but to her surprise the chief justice granted the request.

The Washington *Republican* reported the event, "In the Supreme Court of the United States on Monday, on motion of Mrs. Belva Lockwood, Samuel R. Lowry of Alabama was admitted to practice. Mr. Lowry is president of the Huntsville, Alabama Industrial School and a gentleman of high attainments. It was quite fitting that the first woman admitted to practice before this Court should move the admission of the first Southern colored man. Both will doubtless make good records as representatives of their respective classes."

In June Belva went to Chicago for the Republican Convention. She worked twelve and fourteen hours a day. She secured seats for members of the National Woman Suffrage Association, she worked on a plank that asked for a sixteenth amendment to give women the right to vote, and she talked herself into a meeting of the Committee on Resolutions.

In black velvet trimmed with lace, her dark hair

streaked with gray, she stood before the committee and read: "To the Republican Party in Convention assembled, Chicago, June 2, 1880.

"Seventy-six delegates from local, state and national suffrage associations, representing every section of the United States, are here today to ask you to place the following plank in your platform:

"Resolved: That we pledge ourselves to secure to women the exercise of their right to vote."

She spoke for ten minutes, and finished with, "Your pledge to enfranchise ten millions of women will rouse an enthusiasm which must count in the coming closely contested election. But expendiency is right, and to do justice is ever the highest political wisdom."

But if to do justice was "the highest political wisdom," the delegates to the Republican Convention didn't take advantage of it. In fact, it seemed to Belva that they went out of their way to insult the women whose support they wanted. Chairman Pierrepont of the Platform Committee even went as far as giving Susan B. Anthony ten minutes to plead the women's cause, then held a stop watch ready to strike his gavel when the time expired.

Incidents like these caused many women to leave, but Belva stayed. She found it exciting when the first ballot was taken, and her excitement hadn't diminished when the thirty-sixth ballot was taken and James Garfield won the presidential nomination. Before she returned to Washington, Belva hoped she could come to the next convention.

Belva's fights to enter courts didn't finish with her admittance to the Supreme Court of the United States. Many courts welcomed her, but others weren't so kind. On May 10, 1881, she applied for admittance to the bar of the Carroll County Court at Westminster, Maryland. In her request Belva pointed out that the pronouns *he* and *him* in the codes of the state included all genders. Judge Hayden didn't agree. He said *he* and *him* referred to the masculine only and turned down her request. The *New York Times* said on May 11, "Mrs. Lockwood can practice in the United States District Court of Baltimore and in the Circuit Court of Frederick County in Maryland, but she cannot practice in Judge Hayden's court."

Belva was more fortunate in Massachusetts when she appeared in the United States Circuit Court of that state to argue a cause in equity. As the first woman lawyer to appear before a court in Massachusetts, she was extended every courtesy. Belva wondered publicly what was wrong with some of the judges in Maryland.

Her practice grew through word-of-mouth advertising, through referrals and, of course, through the publicity she received. But it grew also because she was an excellent lawyer. Her clients were always her first concern. She worked long hours. And when work piled up, she hired Lillie Sadler to do the typing so Lura could be free to help do research on the cases. Belva ignored all suggestions that she slow down.

One day when she returned from court Lura told her, "A boy brought a tricycle today. He insisted it belonged here."

Belva ran to the door. Lura followed her. Belva climbed on the high seat and steered the bike erratically down F Street. Lura called, "Mother, what are you doing?"

Belva came back and examined her new mode of transportation. "Lura, do you realize how many miles I walk every day? I rush from one court to another. I'm at the Senate, the House of Representatives. I give speeches all over the city. This tricycle will save me a lot of time."

"Mother, you're not going to ride that thing!"

"Of course I am," Belva said. She climbed on the tricycle and went for another ride.

Belva's new transportation attracted a lot of attention. One reporter wrote, "Strong and healthy in spite of her years, she can make ten miles an hour on the tricycle she rides daily to and from her office."

Belva laughed when she read it. "Ten miles an hour! Not in downtown Washington," she told Lura.

In June 1884 Belva once again represented the women of Washington at the Republican Convention. Once more women fought the delegates' discrimination. At the end of the convention Belva came home furious at the treatment the women had received. Still, despite the insults, Elizabeth Stanton and Susan B. Anthony asked members of the National Woman Suffrage Association to support James Blaine, the Republican's presidential candidate.

Belva decided it was out of the question. On August 10, 1884, she wrote a letter to Susan and sent copies to the editors of different newspapers. One of them was the *Woman's Herald of Industry*, published in California by Marietta L. B. Stow.

She wrote:

> Why not nominate women for important places: Is not Victoria Empress of India? Have we not among our country, women persons of as much talent and ability? Is not history full of precedents of women rulers? The appointment of Phoebe Cousins as assistant marshal of St. Louis is a step in the right direction. It is in keeping with her education and profession, is suitable, legal work, and will have a softening and refining influence on the criminal classes of the

city of St. Louis, and the attachés of the court. There should be more appointments of the same sort.

If women in the states are not permitted to vote, there is no law against their being voted for, and if elected, filling the highest office in the gift of the people.

Two of the present political parties who have candidates in the field believe in woman suffrage. It would have been well had some of the candidates been women. There is no use in attempting to avoid the inevitable.

The Republican party, claiming to be the party of progress, has little else but insult for women, when they appear before its "conventions" and ask for recognition. Note, for instance, the resolution on woman suffrage presented to their convention on June 5.

It is quite time that we had our own party; our own platform, and our own nominees.

We shall never have equal rights until we take them, nor respect until we command it. Act up to your convictions of justice and right, and you cannot go far wrong.

Yours truly,
Belva A. Lockwood

On September 25, 1884, she received a letter from San Francisco. It said:

170

Madame, we the undersigned, have the honor to congratulate you as the first woman ever nominated for the highest office in the gift of a nation, and we further congratulate you upon the cordial manner in which the nomination has been received by both people and press.

It was signed by Clara S. Foltz, Mary J. Holt, Elizabeth J. Corbett, M. D., and Marietta L. Stow.

Belva re-read the letter. She sat at her desk stunned. She had just become a candidate for the Presidency of the United States.

Chapter Fourteen

*B*elva *didn't say* anything to anyone about the nomination. She thought somebody might be playing a joke on her, but investigation revealed that Marietta Stow had added comments of her own when she printed Belva's letter in her newspaper, then sent copies to women around the country. Their reaction had prompted the women of California to call a convention where they nominated Belva for the leading office in the country and Marietta Stow as her running mate.

Three days after Belva received the letter, she went to the District Supreme Court to file two civil cases. "Good morning, Clancy," she said to the assistant clerk.

"Good morning, Mrs. Lockwood." The man took her papers and examined them. He signed them and placed his seal next to his name. "Say, Mrs. Lockwood, you ought to vote for Ben Butler, the Labor Party candidate," Clancy said.

"I don't have a vote, Clancy."

"I was just teasing. But if you had a vote, you would cast it for him, wouldn't you? He's the ideal man for your cause," the clerk said.

Belva fingered the paper in her pocket. Lura and DeForest didn't even know about the nomination. But Belva couldn't keep silent any longer, "Clancy, I have a nomination myself," she said.

The clerk laughed while he read the letter. "That's the best joke of the season," he said.

"It's not a joke, Clancy. I have the acceptance in my pocket. But you mustn't tell anyone." She pointed to the reporter assigned to cover the courthouse. "Especially him. My daughter doesn't know about it yet."

"I won't tell anyone, Mrs. Lockwood," Clancy said. Belva heard him chuckling as she walked toward the door.

She rode her tricycle to the post office to mail her letter to California, then rode to the Court of Claims to file cases and stopped at the War Department to check on a claim for a client. By the time Belva reached her office, Lura had heard about the nomination and so had the press.

A reporter from the *Evening Critic* was waiting for her. "Mrs. Lockwood, I hear you have a nomination for the Presidency. The *Critic* would like a copy of it and the reply," he said.

Belva said, "You can't have the original letter, and I only have rough notes of my acceptance. But I suppose Miss Sadler can make a copy for you," she said. She handed the papers to her typist.

The reporter asked, "What will your platform be?"

"I have notes on that too, but I'm not ready to release them. I'll see that you get a copy when I am," Belva said.

Before Lillie finished the notes, another reporter came in. "Mrs. Lockwood, we hear that you have accepted a nomination for the Presidency. We must have the story," the man said. Once more Lillie Sadler typed from the notes. After he left, Belva answered Lura's questions.

Lura said, "Mother, you never cease to amaze me." Belva smiled and went to her room to get ready for a concert.

When she returned home a reporter from the *National Republican* was sitting on her front stoop. He asked for the story. This time Belva had her platform ready. She told him about it.

"That's an ambitious platform," the reporter said.

"Women have to be ambitious if they're going to get any place."

After the man left Belva reviewed the events of the day. When she had awakened that morning, she had wondered what to do with the nomination. Now, she knew she would go out and campaign the way the candidates of the major parties did. People would laugh. But they had done that before. She knew that the National Equal Rights Party had little chance of winning the highest office in the land. But there had to be a step in that direction some day, and she was taking it.

Belva had expected help from the National Woman Suffrage Association, but she didn't get it. Within days after her story appeared in the newspapers, she received a letter from Susan B. Anthony telling her that the association never supported a candidate from a minor party. Belva was disappointed but not defeated. She set up a schedule of personal appearances and speeches that kept her exhausted, but let the public know that her efforts were sincere.

The newspaper people were kind when they weren't being humorous. A farcical piece appeared in the *New York Times*, which annoyed Lura, but which made Belva laugh. The article "accused" her of using false hair in the back of her head. The writer said she had once bribed a justice of the peace with caramels. And, of course, he had to mention the style of the skirts. The article went on:

> The divided-skirt question is now depriving Mrs. Lockwood of sleep. As is well known many of the women who advocate woman's suffrage wear skirts of the ordinary pattern, while others wear either the divided skirts or trousers. If Mrs. Lockwood pledges herself to support the great divided-skirt reform she will receive the enthusiastic support of the divided-skirt wearers, but she will lose the confidence of the wearers of ordinary skirts with an opposite but equally disastrous result that will follow any act on her part which openly identified her with the ordinary-skirt party. For some days the woman's suffrage women have anxiously waited for Mrs. Lockwood to commit herself on the divided-skirt question, but as yet she has refrained from doing so.

Lura asked her mother, "Why do they write such things? You should complain to the editor."

"They're not hurting me. Besides, I'm a public figure, and I'm fair game for the press," Belva said.

However, in October when she held interviews with the New York reporters in her rooms at the Fifth Avenue Hotel, Belva teased them about their stories. "You're our most interesting candidate, Mrs. Lock-

wood," one man said. "People want to read about you."

A reporter asked Belva's manager, Brad Adams, "Will you vote for Mrs. Lockwood, Mr. Adams?"

"I'm a Grover Cleveland man," he said. "But I think Mrs. Lockwood is a brave woman, and I want to help her."

"Doesn't it bother you to have a Grover Cleveland man working for you, Mrs. Lockwood?" someone asked.

"I hired him because he's a good manager. I'm not interested in his politics," Belva said smiling.

She heard music outside. Everyone crowded around the windows. Two horses pulled a truck that carried a muslin frame with these inscriptions: "National Equal Rights Party; The Next President Belva A. Lockwood; Academy of Music, Sunday Evening."

Belva said to her manager, "Keep that thing riding up and down Broadway and Fifth Avenue all day. I want a crowd at the academy tomorrow night." She got one. She usually did. In fact, she was continuously amazed at the large crowds who came to hear her and gave her their attention. They helped her tolerate the hecklers.

After the speech at the Academy of Music, Belva went back to Washington and took care of several legal cases, then went on the road again. By election eve she was back in Washington, delivering speeches around the city. At each meeting she stressed her platform. She told her audiences: "I promise equal rights for all citizens without distinction of color, sex or nationality. I promise aid for lagging industries and better trade relations with our South American neighbors. I oppose monopolies that make the rich richer and leave the poor in a position of virtual slavery. I shall ask for better educational opportunities for everyone, and I shall insist that the government make Indians citizens and let them rule their personal affairs."

On election day Belva went to the polls with DeForest while he cast his ballot. People recognized her. She shook hands and answered their questions. Then she conducted her legal business as though this weren't the most exciting day in her life.

Grover Cleveland won the election. Belva accepted defeat graciously, but she wouldn't accept the election results with the same grace. When election clerks wouldn't acknowledge her claim of more votes, she asked Senator Hoar to introduce a petition in Congress. It stated that she had received 3,149 votes and the entire electoral vote of Indiana. Besides these votes Belva Lockwood and Marietta Stow claimed half the electoral vote of Oregon and the hundreds of votes in Pennsylvania that had been dumped into the wastebaskets as false votes.

179

The day after Senator Hoar filed Belva's petition, Lura said to Belva, "It's too bad you lost, Mother. I'd like being the President's daughter."

Belva laughed. "I didn't lose." Lura looked at Belva questioningly. "I set a precedent. And every time a woman sets a precedent, she wins a victory."

Belva stuffed folders in her suitcase. She was due in court in twenty minutes.

Epilogue

In 1885 *Belva* wrote and presented to Congress a bill asking for an international court to preserve peace in the world. As a result of her work, she was sent to Europe by the State Department to attend the Congress of Charities in Geneva, Switzerland. From there she went to the Seventh International Peace Congress in Hungary where she presented a paper titled "Civil and Political Life of Woman in the United States."

In 1887 Belva Lockwood, Attorney-at-Law, became Belva A. Lockwood and Company, Attorneys-at-Law, when Lura and a woman named Clara B. Harrison joined Belva in her court cases. Their assistance gave Belva more time to devote to her outside interests.

In 1888 the women of Iowa made Belva a candidate

for the Presidency once more. This time Alfred Love was her running mate. In the election Belva fared no better than she had in 1884. That was fine with her. Even before the results were in, she had decided to leave politics to others while she devoted more time to peace.

She was a member of the Universal Peace Union. She became president of the National Arbitration Society and secretary of the American Branch of the International Peace Bureau. In 1889 she went to Paris for the International Peace Congress where she delivered a speech on international arbitration. And in 1890 she went to London to present a paper on disarmament to the delegates of the Peace Congress assembled in Westminster Hall. When the meetings ended, Belva stayed in England. Always curious, always searching, she took a course of lectures at Oxford University.

After she returned to the states, Jim Taylor, a Cherokee Indian, for whom Belva had conducted several cases, came to see her. He told her that he had convinced his people to let her handle their long-standing claim against the government. Belva felt overwhelmed by the trust and by the work that trust represented.

She knew about the claim that had arisen shortly after the signing of the Treaty of New Echota in 1835 by the Cherokees and the government of the United States. She knew also that the treaty had called for the removal of the Cherokee Indians from North Carolina and the purchase of their land by the government. And the difference between the parties had grown and magnified until another treaty was signed. But the new document didn't resolve the problems of the Cherokee.

Belva studied the treaties Jim Taylor brought. Within days she made a trip to North Carolina to talk to descendants of the original signers of the Treaty of New Echota. She returned often to go over facts and to get affidavits from the thousands of people involved. She realized from her visits that the case wouldn't take weeks or months. It would take years. It would all have to be worked into her crowded calendar.

In 1894 Lura died after a brief illness. The loss left Belva numb. Still, she went on with her work for peace. She continued her trips to North Carolina and made several to Indian country in the West. She went to Europe to another Peace Congress. Life had to go on as it had after the deaths of the others she had loved.

And when several of her friends asked her to help them with a Married Woman's Property Rights Bill, Belva started making notes the same day. Together, the women came up with a bill that provided a fair inheritance law for married women. Also, it gave them

rights to bargain, sell and convey property, to enter into contract, to sue, to carry on business. Most important, however, the bill gave the women the right of guardianship.

A man could no longer throw his wife out of his house and keep the children unless he could prove she was an unfit mother. After President William McKinley signed the law on June 1, 1896, Belva presented an embossed copy of the new statute to the women of the National Woman Suffrage Association. Thousands of women had been freed from the slavery of a discriminating law.

The beginning of the new century found Belva still working on the Cherokee case. It reached the United States Court of Claims during the winter term of 1903. Judge Nott presided. Belva felt the excitement of a winner when he agreed that the government owed her clients monies. However, she wasn't satisfied with the amount he was willing to award.

Belva felt the Cherokees were entitled to more money. She took the case to the Supreme Court of the United States. There, she won five million dollars for her clients. And for herself she won the satisfaction of proving to Judge Charles C. Nott that not only did a woman have the legal capacity to take the office of attorney, she had the ability to do the job well. Her triumph was reported throughout the country.

Though she was nearing her seventy-sixth birthday in 1906, Belva represented the International League of Press Clubs and the Universal Union at the International Peace Congress in Milan, Italy. In 1908 she made another trip abroad in the name of peace. At home she continued her work until a few months before her death. Belva died in the George Washington University Hospital on May 19, 1917.

Belva Ann Lockwood never voted. However, the right she sought was finally granted to women when the Nineteenth Amendment became part of the Constitution of the United States on August 26, 1920. In an article about her, the Washington *Star* wrote, "While the worthy claims of others are being extolled for their part in securing the passage of the Nineteenth Amendment to the Constitution of the United States, the people of Washington, of all people in the country, must certainly not overlook the invaluable work of Belva Ann Lockwood."

Belva herself wrote in *Lippincott's Monthly Magazine* in February 1888, "I never stopped fighting. My cause was the cause of thousands of women."

The Nineteenth Amendment proved she fought her cause well.